I0027197

African Conflicts, Development and Regional Organisations in the Post-Cold War International System

The Annual Claude Ake Memoral Lecture
Uppsala, Sweden 30 January 2014

Victor A.O. Adetula, PhD

… [the] international peace and security system requires a network of actors with a broad set of capacities, so that regional organisations can undertake peace operations in situations where the UN is unable to do so. (Bam 2012: 8)

NORDISKA AFRIKAINSTITUTET, UPPSALA 2015

INDEXING TERMS:
Conflicts
Dispute settlement
Peacebuilding
Regional organizations
Regional integration
Conflict management
Regional security
International security
Africa

ISSN 0280-2171
ISBN 978-91-7106-765-4
© The author, The Nordic Africa Institute, Uppsala University and
the Department of Peace and Conflict Research
Production: Byrå4
Print on demand, Lightning Source UK Ltd.

Contents

This is No. 8 in the CAMP series, the series of research reports presenting the printed version of the Claude Ake Memorial Lectures given at end of a longer research stay at Uppsala University and the Nordic Africa Institute by the annual holder of the Claude Ake Visiting Chair.

This Claude Ake Memorial Lecture was delivered by Professor Victor A.O. Adetula on January 30, 2014. Dr. Adetula is Professor of International Relations and Development Studies at the University of Jos, Nigeria and Head of Division of Africa and Regional Integration at the Nigerian Institute of International Affairs, Lagos. In his lecture Dr. Adetula discussed the armed conflicts confronting the African nations, their connections to development and the possibilities for establishing peace with the use of regional and continental governmental organizations. His lecture provides the reader with a comprehensive overview of the predicaments facing Africa and its conflict management experiences. He reports achievements as well as setbacks. He also appeals to African leaders to strengthen their support for the structures that now are in place, politically as well as financially.

It is my belief that this lecture is important for all students of African affairs, and, thus, is happy to include it in the series of distinguished lectures. As is customary to note, this publication constitutes the work of the author and does not necessarily reflect the views of the host institutions.

Uppsala, Sweden, November 2014

Peter Wallensteen
Professor, Department of Peace and Conflict Research
Nordic Africa Institute Associate and CAMP Series Editor

Preamble and appreciation

This lecture is to celebrate Professor Claude Ake, who was easily one of the best scholars of African development. He was a distinguished social scientist and an unparalleled development theorist whose contributions will remain a subject of intellectual discourse among Africanists for a very long time. The theme of today's lecture connects to Ake's scholarship and personality in many ways, two of which I wish to highlight. First, Ake's final intellectual endeavours focused on the roots of political violence in Africa. Second, this platform provides me with a long-desired opportunity to publicly acknowledge Ake's influence on my career.

I first met the late scholar in 1992 at a conference entitled "Democratic Transition in Africa" at the University of Ibadan (Nigeria) where, as a keynote speaker, he eloquently queried the feasibility of liberal democracy in Africa. In 1995, when I met him the second time, he was on the review panel of the John D. and Catherine T. MacArthur Foundation. The Foundation later encouraged me to study Ake's modes of engagement on the Niger Delta question. Our last meeting was in 1996 in his office-cum-library at the Centre for Advanced Social Science, Port Harcourt. I had gone to see him to draw lessons that could help me develop appropriate political economy frameworks for studying the social and economic impact of environmental degradation in the tin mining areas of Jos Plateau. Professor Ake died only a few days later. Until now, the only way in which I memorialised Ake's impact on my scholarship was through a compilation of tributes to him, published by the African Centre for Democratic Governance (Adetula 1997).

Holding the chair that honours Professor Claude Ake has indeed offered me an opportunity to reconnect with him! For this, I thank Uppsala University and the Nordic Africa Institute, and indeed the Swedish government for supporting the establishment of the Claude Ake Visiting Chair in the Department of Peace and Conflict Research, Uppsala University. I am aware of a number of institutions in Africa where public lectures have been inaugurated in memory of Professor Ake. However, the establishment of visiting fellowships for the study of Africa in honour of the late sage is a unique demonstration of international cooperation. I am particularly delighted to be in the company of the eminent scholars who previously held this chair, and it is on behalf of all of us that I say a big thank you once again to both the Department of Peace and Conflict Research and the Nordic Africa Institute for providing us with a conducive setting for research and knowledge-sharing on Africa.

A number of recent studies have expressed marked optimism about the constant decrease in armed conflicts around the world. One such study projects that by 2050 the proportion of countries at war will have declined significantly, with high prospects for global peace and security (Hegre et al. 2013). Using Uppsala Conflict Data Program (UCDP) data, Hegre et al. associate the long years of peace enjoyed in the world with decreased global poverty, and project that the trend is likely to continue into the future. The prognosis shows that many countries in the world will remain peaceful in coming years. It is, however, noted that countries with high poverty, low education and young populations are fertile ground for conflict, and that more than half the world's conflicts during 2012 occurred in such countries. The prognosis for Africa does not reflect the same optimism. Poverty reduction, transparent and accountable governance and citizen satisfaction with the delivery of public goods and service have shown no sign of significant improvement. In consequence, peace has continued to elude the continent, and this trend may continue unless radical measures are taken to prevent further deterioration within a holistic and integrated strategy that emphasises democratic governance, economic development and equitable distribution of wealth as conditions for peace and security.

Civil war is a constant threat in many poor and badly governed countries in Africa. However, the causal relationship between armed conflict and underdevelopment is complex. Thus, analyses and prognoses that link conflict and underdevelopment require qualification. Recent studies suggest that "while ... it seems plausible that poverty can create the desperation that fuels conflict, the precise ... causal linkage is not quite evident. There are poor societies that are remarkably peaceful, and richer societies that are mired in violence" (Östby 2013: 207). Africa is reported to have made "impressive progress in addressing other development challenges" since the beginning of the millennium in terms of economic growth rate, which was the highest in the world; improved business environment and investment climate; and a rapidly expanding labour force (Ascher and Mirovitskaya 2013: 3). Nonetheless, the continent still faces some of the most daunting global security threats. For example, 29 (40 per cent) of the 73 state-based conflicts active in 2002-11 were in Africa (Themnér and Wallensteen 2013: 47). Also, of the 223 non-state conflicts in 2002-11, 165 (some 73 per cent) were in Africa, and mostly in Ethiopia, Kenya, Nigeria, Somalia and Sudan, which between them accounted for 125 of the non-state conflicts (Themnér and Wallensteen 2013: 52). In 2011, Africa recorded several significant internationalised intrastate conflicts, some of them of long standing (Allansson et al. 2013: 17). During this period, new conflicts erupted in Libya, Sudan and South Sudan. Also, dormant conflicts in Côte d'Ivoire and Senegal became active. The situation in northern Mali remains a threat just as the deadly conflicts in the Central Africa Republic (CAR) and Libya are fast escalating into civil war. In East Africa, for many years the activities of al-Shabaab militants have made Somalia and the entire sub-region unsafe. In Democratic Republic of Congo (DRC), the military defeat of the M23 rebel movement has not brought lasting peace, mainly because of the almost complete absence of a functioning state.

Armed conflicts in Africa, and particularly intra-state conflicts, have attracted the attention of the international community, which has responded by supporting various peace initiatives. A significant number of multilateral peace-keeping and peace operations have been launched to address African conflicts. By the end of 2013, eight of the UN's 15 peacekeeping missions were in Africa, and involved 70 per cent of all UN peacekeepers deployed globally (Ladsous 2014). Despite this level of multilateral intervention, only limited impacts have been recorded. While one can argue that the number and intensity of armed conflicts has declined in Africa, violence by armed non-state actors is on the increase. Ongoing armed insurgencies in Nigeria and parts of the Sahel, notably Mali and Niger, best illustrate this trend, with several deaths recorded. In addition, organised crime is on the rise across the continent, coupled with the emergence of new forms of violence associated with contemporary globalisation and other post-Cold War phenomena.

The post-Westphalian international system introduced new challenges that have implications for global peace and stability, particularly for the most vulnerable regions of the world. With the end of the Cold War, the international system lost its highly structured "framework within which the internal and international behaviour of Third World states was regulated" (Snow 1996: 4). Donald Snow adds that "the end of the Cold War has been accompanied by an apparently reduced willingness and ability to control internal violence ... Governments and potential insurgents no longer have ideological patrons who provided them with the wherewithal to commit violence and then expect some influence over how that violence is carried out" (Snow 1996: 46). These developments introduced "greater instability" that increases "the likelihood of the outbreak of violent conflict and opening the doors of atrocities." Added to these are forms of violence that are partly enhanced by the "end of bi-polar Cold War stability" and "the fundamental changes in the social relations governing the ways in which wars are fought" (Melander et al. 2006: 9). Global illicit trade in drugs, arms and weapons; human trafficking; piracy etc. are now part of the threat to global peace and international security.

The international system is presently resting on fragmented global governance foundations. The multilateral system is not working that well, despite the rhetoric by states in support of global cooperative responses. Neither the Bretton Woods-UN system nor informal plurilateral bodies such as the Group of Eight

(G8) and G20 Leaders' Summits have demonstrated the potential or capacity to help Africa and other vulnerable regions in overcoming global pressures. For instance, while Africa and the challenges of development feature regularly on the agendas of international organisations and development partners, commitments to assist the continent are generally accompanied by new conditionalities and other criteria that are justified under the new discourse on aid effectiveness and aid for trade. With the end of the Cold War, powerful and rich countries of the global North redefined their national interests and reorganised them in less altruistic ways that seem not to emphasise cooperative initiatives. Meanwhile, the world is being treated to the emergence of new global powers, notably Brazil, Russia, India and China (BRIC). The BRIC states are increasingly involved in global issues such as trade, international security, climate change and energy politics. However, while they have shown an interest in global issues, they are not necessarily prepared to assume responsibility for international development, including global peace and security. These developments provide opportunities for regional actors to become more engaged in developing and expanding their roles in conflict management and maintaining regional security.

The strengthening of regional organisations and the emergence of new regional networks are important features of the post-Cold War system. Regional institutions are becoming increasingly prominent in contemporary international relations. The complexity of security challenges in the post-bipolar world requires greater cooperation and coordination among states within a region. Current waves of globalisation are already promoting regional consensus-formation and coordination. The inability of many national governments to address problems with cross-border dimensions, such as pests, desertification, drought, climate change, HIV/AIDS, drug and human trafficking has further encouraged states to embrace regionalist approaches. Both in the areas of economic development and security, many states now favour regional organisations and other forms of alliance. These organisations have become more associated with the task and responsibility of maintaining world peace. In this context, the emergence of the African Union (AU), for instance, represents a renewed commitment by African states to a regional approach.

Dominant international relations discourse in the post-Cold War era acknowledges "complex interdependence" as one of the defining characteristics of the global system and tends to favour a regionalist approach to the management of inter-state relations. There are still challenges at various levels – national, regional and global. For example, some states are still protective of their sovereignty despite the overwhelming impact of globalisation and the attacks on the territorial state. Regionally, many organisations have serious capacity gaps. And globally, there are, among other things, the challenges of power politics. In this lecture, I examine the performance of Africa's regional organisations in ensuring peace and security on the continent. In doing this, I draw attention to the need for national and regional actors to pay attention to good governance and development as part of their efforts to operate effective collective security systems and conflict resolution mechanisms without ignoring the essence of the global context.

Conceptually, conflict, conflict resolution and peacebuilding are represented in this lecture as parts of the development process (Adetula 2005). Also, the dominant conception of security is aligned with the notion of human security. I thus deliberately set aside the restricted statist notion of security. The focus on state power and interests is unquestionably the contribution of the realists, whose prominence in the development of contemporary international relations theory and practice has remained almost incontestable. Despite the increasingly interdependent character of inter-state relations in the modern state system, the statist notion of security has significantly influenced the evolution, goals and directions of international organisations. Consequently, collective security systems – regional and global – first emerged out of concerns for the security of states and in defence of states rather than people. Today, the discourse on collective security system is moving to accommodate consideration of the people as the focus of all security arrangements, hence the infusion of human security into collective security systems.

In the words of Necla Tschirgi: "The concept of peace-building – bridging security and development at the international and domestic levels – came to offer an integrated approach to understanding and dealing with the full range of issues that threatened peace and security" (2003: 1). In this framework, key peacebuilding considerations include the prevention and resolution of violent conflicts, consolidation of peace once violence has been reduced and post-conflict reconstruction with a view to avoiding relapses into violent conflict. These new conceptions transcend the traditional military, diplomatic and security approaches of the Cold War to include how to address "the proximate and root causes of contemporary conflicts including structural, political, socio-cultural, economic and environmental factors" (Tschirgi 2003: 1). Tschirgi's comment on the connection between development and security is apt:

> Not all development impacts the security environment. Conversely, not all security concerns have ramifications for development. Where the two come together – to cause, perpetuate, reduce, prevent or manage violent conflicts – is the appropriate terrain for peace-building ... [P]eace-building requires a willingness to rethink the traditional boundaries between these two domains and to expand these boundaries to include ... defense budgets, international trade and finance, natural resource management and international governance ... Peace-building also requires a readiness to change the operations and mandates of existing political, security, and development establishments. Most importantly, it requires the ability to make a difference on the ground in preventing violent conflicts or establishing the conditions for a return to sustainable peace. (2003: 1).

The literature on African development is generally rich. However, the dominant conception of development in Africa sees it in a strictly economic sense. Within this restricted economistic view, some development theorists and practitioners give little or no consideration to political issues. The challenges of development are scarcely defined and analysed beyond how to guarantee efficiency in management and increase productivity. Thus, no effort is made to address broad social and political questions that are central to conflict. This failure to appreciate that development involves the totality of human and societal affairs, and cannot (and should not) be restricted to the economic sphere is a major conceptual and theoretical deficiency (Adetula 2014).

Broad conceptualisations of development provide the foundation for a key hypothesis in the following presentation: namely, the crisis of African development is at the root of the incessant armed conflict on the continent. In Africa, the failure of the postcolonial state to establish a political order, both as a necessary condition for accumulation and for enhancing legitimation, has resulted in pervasive disorder and instability on the continent. Africa today presents a pitiable catalogue of conflicts with negative consequences for development. Interestingly, knowledge of the link between armed conflict and development is gradually advancing, resulting in the emergence of new conceptions of the relationship between security and development. African countries have mostly responded by collectively promoting sub-regional and continental initiatives on conflict resolution and peacebuilding. Admittedly, the many violent conflicts in Africa and their domino effect at the sub-regional level have contributed to the desire for regional collective security and conflict-management mechanisms.

Many African countries are either embroiled in conflict or have just emerged from it. There is scarcely any part of Africa without its share of major conflict, either ongoing or recently resolved. It is possible to identify conflicts of secession, of ethnic sub-nationalism, self-determination, military intervention, and over citizenship and land ownership (see Table 1). The dominant perspective in the literature is of armed conflict characterising the political process in African states. Also, until recently very little attention has been paid to regional and global dynamics in terms of the way they interact with the causes, conduct and resolution of armed conflicts in Africa.

Another observable trend is a plethora of empirical data on the "rates" and "indexes" of violence in Africa. It is not my intention to argue against the relevance of such quantitative analysis of African conflicts. However, suffice it to point out that concentrating on rates and indexes may oversimplify the issues, "leading to ignorance of and little consideration for what some felt were 'low intensity conflicts'" (Tandia 2012: 37). It is important to stress here that focusing on macro-indicators such as "deaths per year" encourages over-subscription to the Weberian notion of state and order. This comes with the risk of concealing other important indicators of political violence that have not become popular with regional organisations and inter-governmental institutions as criteria to justify intervention. This is not helpful to understanding the character and dynamics of African conflicts. Rather, both quantitative and qualitative methods are useful:

> When reliable data are available and cautiously compiled, objectives of the study are carefully stated and research design is consistent with these objectives and data limitations, quantitative studies can provide useful insights, especially if complemented and reinforced by quantitative methods that help "observe the unobservable," such as group motivations, types of leadership, political connections, and other context-specific factors. (Ascher and Mirovitskaya 2013: 6)

African conflicts and the resultant security challenges continue to be of utmost concern to the international community. The complexity of these inter-related processes cannot be easily denied. It is interesting that scholars of African conflicts, particularly in the post-Cold War period, are moving away from the previous state-centric perspective. Also, the perspective that African conflicts are often related to the crisis of the African state is fast gaining prominence (Ohlson 2012). However, there is as yet no viable single theory that explains the occurrence and consequences of armed violence in contemporary Africa. Neither the theory of underdevelopment cum dependency, nor the frustration and aggression hypothesis, nor the Collier–Hoeffler dichotomy of greed vs. grievance adequately explain the realities of African conflicts, especially after the Cold War. For instance, it is no longer plausible to argue for a positive correlation between high ethnic diversity and frequent sectarian violence. Ascher and Mirovitskaya (2013: 3) point out that in many African countries "ethnic, religious, or regional divisions have little relevance in defining the basis for intergroup violence, although they may be mobilized if conflict arises for other reasons." They also show that "deep rooted poverty is not a predictor of large-scale violence either, as many African countries at very low levels of development remained peaceful for decades."

Similarly, the assumption that liberal democracy will promote good governance and hence reduce violent conflicts in Africa has been challenged (Adetula 2011). Most African countries have from the 1990s transitioned from authoritarian rule to various forms of democratic government. The reintroduction of multiparty politics has not changed the nature of governance in many African countries and has therefore had little or no effect in mitigating violent conflict. Electoral politics have indeed generated many contradictions for most of the young democracies, which are now experiencing mixed political outcomes, often including violent political conflict. Electoral competition has produced undesirable results that threaten peace and security in Nigeria, Côte d'Ivoire, Kenya and Zimbabwe, to name just a few cases. Conflict erupted in Côte d'Ivoire in the early 2000s, and dragged on until 2010 when presidential elections were held. The disputes over election outcomes further intensified the conflict and led to large-scale violence that attracted international responses. Moreover, coup d'états in Guinea-Bissau and Mali were linked to electoral competitions. In the case of Mali, Tuareg and Salafist insurgents in the north capitalised on the instability created by the military takeover of government to further their demands for secession. It would be unwise to ignore or downplay democracy in the quest for peace and political stability in Africa. However, there is still much to learn about the social, economic and political contexts of African conflicts. Thus, I have adopted a hybrid model that considers many variables in intra-state armed conflict in Africa, including regional dynamics.

State failure continues to drive many violent conflicts in Africa. The continent provides many examples of "ineffective, dysfunctional or non-existent" states that are unable to function as such (Bruck 2013: 2). In addition, they constitute security threats to their populations and neighbours. Such states are not only incapable of delivering a democracy and promoting economic development, they are unable to secure their territories because they are unable to monopolise violence or prevent its use by non-state insurgents and criminal groups, as is the case in Somalia, CAR and Libya. Also, because of weak governance in Africa, the benefits of natural resource endowments have continually bypassed most people in Africa, despite reported growth and rising incomes. For instance, large rents accruing to African countries with mineral resources such as Nigeria, DRC, Angola and Gabon, have not narrowed social disparities among their populations. Development policies and programmes in many of these countries have not resulted in the distribution of wealth in favour of the majority.

Coupled with the lack of effective conflict resolution mechanisms, horizontal inequalities or inequalities among identity groups, and feelings of marginalisation have intensified political conflicts in many multi-ethnic or multi-religious African societies. Nzongoa-Ntalaja warns that "a transformation is not possible in situations of violent conflicts and/or those in which the institutions and processes of governance are unresponsive, unaccountable, or simply ineffective" (2002). The existence of many new and renewed wars in Africa is linked to "bad governments and stagnant economies," which in turn impoverish and alienate the people. The Arab Spring helps us appreciate that poverty is at the root of discontent in many conflict-ridden countries (Acemoglu and Robinson 2013: 1).

Despite increased growth rates in Africa, there has been no corresponding reduction in poverty (Dulani 2013). In 2012, the continent reportedly had 24 countries with greater inequality than China. Poverty has not only reduced the ability of the population to lead productive lives, it has also exacerbated identity conflicts along communal, ethnic, religious and regional lines. As the living conditions of most citizens in Africa countries deteriorate, many have become more attached to primordial ties and less committed to supporting governments. For instance, poverty has continued to aggravate tensions among groups in some parts of Nigeria, where the "citizenship or nationality question" has degenerated into sectarian violence. Despite Nigeria's vast natural resources, about half the population lives in poverty (World Bank 2013). Closer examination reveals regional differences, which partly explain perceptions of inequality and marginalisation along regional lines.[1] Incessant violence in parts of the country, notably youth militancy in the Niger Delta and Islamic insurgency in the northeast, can be related to the horizontal inequalities in Nigeria.

African conflicts are mostly protracted and intractable, some lasting up to two decades. "Conflict trap" logic partly explains why countries that have experienced civil war most of the time relapse into it. Incessant conflict in DRC and to some extent Côte d'Ivoire exemplifies this logic. In many cases, a few months after conflicts are settled in these countries, they recur usually in another form. This has been attributed to the "negative economic growth" typical of post-conflict societies, whose indicators include low GDP, widespread unemployment, a thriving underground economy, poor public health and high levels of inequality and insecurity (Kreutz 2012).

---

1. The overall average poverty rate for Nigeria is 48.3 per cent (based on an adult equivalent approach). The rate for the northeast is 59.7 per cent, northwest 58 per cent, north-central 48.8 per cent, southeast 39 per cent, south 37. 6 per cent and southwest 30.6 per cent.

The cyclical nature of many African conflicts has been partly blamed on weak political institutions, including those responsible for conflict resolution, whose ineffectiveness is already common knowledge. In these circumstances, conflict management mechanisms yield no positive and lasting outcomes, as interventions are mostly short-term. The peace process in DRC exhibited these characteristics (Nyuykonge 2012). The depth of antagonism between the DRC government and the UN Stabilisation Mission (MONUSCO) on one hand, and rebel movements on the other, has been implicated in the failure of the DRC peace process. This situation creates daunting challenges for post-conflict recovery and a high prospect of renewed conflict. Characteristically, prolonged violence weakens state institutions and structures, usually giving rise in their stead to a plethora of informal networks connected with governance structures and privately with the economy (Utas 2012). The growth of "more influential and stronger informal governance" has made peacebuilding and state-building in post-conflict societies very difficult, as witness Liberia and Sierra Leone. The "big men" and informal networks produced by African conflicts usually wield significant influence in conflict zones, especially in the absence of state institutions. This complicates peacebuilding and contributes greatly to the intractability of violent conflict on the continent. Examples abound in Africa of the difficulties and challenges associated with rebuilding formal institutions of governance in post-conflict societies.

This rebuilding requires a comprehensive and integrated recovery programme to help bring about efficient governance that can in turn aid peacebuilding. In addition, these processes must be complemented by organised reconciliation and reconstruction. There are serious budgetary implications. Past experience in Africa shows that such recovery programmes are mostly funded by donors, which make them vulnerable to political interference and overly bureaucratic. In these situations, the peace process has been seriously threatened, and in some instances fresh conflicts have ensued, as in Liberia and Sierra Leone. The outbreak of fresh violence in South Sudan also illustrates the consequences of "a flawed peace process." The implementation of the comprehensive peace agreement has not lead to positive transformation to the benefit of the generality of citizens, who still feel alienated and marginalised (Young 2012).

The political settlement in post-conflict Sierra Leone is another case in point. While some present Sierra Leone as a success story, there are concerns that failure to address fundamental issues of access to power, accountability in the control of natural resources and extreme poverty may result in marginalisation, disenfranchisement and new forms of violence (Allouche 2014). Similarly, armed conflict in northern Mali calls for more caution in the management of the peace process. Although military efforts led by the French have quelled the armed violence, and the country has gone through processes culminating in the inauguration of its newly elected president, Ibrahim Boubacar Keïta, a lasting solution requires a much broader peacebuilding process beyond the deployment of the UN peace mission in northern Mali. Much remains to be done to ensure sustainable peace and security.

Regional context has become more pronounced in armed conflicts and African conflicts are not excepted. In Africa, the idea that "all Africans are the same" enhances the regional dimension of conflicts. The region harbours people of common history, traditions and customs separated by national boundaries under the modern state system. For illustration, the Bantu and Khoisan and Xhosa are spread across Southern Africa just as the Masai and Somali are distributed across Djibouti, Ethiopia, Kenya and Somali. The Arabs are a significant presence in Mauritania, Morocco, Western Sahara and Tunisia. Hausa and Fulbe are widely spoken in Nigeria, Niger, Cameroon, Senegal, Mali and Ghana. Also in West Africa, Liberia, Sierra Leone and Guinea lie within the Mano River area and share membership in the Mano River Union. When Charles Taylor of Liberia launched his rebellion near the Guinea/Liberia/Sierra Leone border, Sierra Leone and Guinea bore the brunt of the refugee influx. The conflict subsequently spilled over into Sierra Leone. Similarly, the presence of Sierra Leonean rebel forces along the border with Guinea and Liberia led to the spill-over of violence into those countries, and the growth of region-wide conflict. Taylor's Liberia supported Sierra Leonean and Guinean rebels while Guinea backed Liberian rebels. According to Wallensteen, data show "that neighbouring countries are not only affected by refugee flows, disruption flows, disruption of transportation routes and smuggling of weapons. Governments may support particular opposition groups on the other side of the border. One government may align itself with the neighbouring government against particular rebel groups" (2012: 3). In Africa, there are many examples of conflict starting in one area and engulfing the entire region. Awareness of the relationship between environmental change and armed conflict is being expanded to include the implications for regional peace and security. Several million people have fled their homes as a result of war, crime, riots, political unrest, floods, earthquakes, volcanoes, typhoons, forms of climate change and other causes. While Liberia and Sierra Leone deal with the aftermath of conflict and try to rebuild, other countries in West Africa like Nigeria and Niger experience environment-related conflicts between, for instance, farmers and herders, over access to scarce environmental resources, and destabilising population movements. Africa's physical and demographic features and the porosity of its borders make it easy for environment-induced conflicts to assume regional character. It is in this context that climate change, desertification, famine and drought are considered threats to regional peace and security in West, East and Central Africa. In West Africa, the expansion of agricultural activities by the various communities is putting more pressure on land and other environmental resources. The same is true of East Africa, especially the Great Lakes region, where water-related conflicts have become an almost everyday occurrence. Consequently, intercommunal and sometimes inter-state relations have become more conflict-ridden. There is, however, new evidence that resource scarcity is not sufficient, in itself, to cause violence. When such scarcity does contribute to violence, it always interacts with other political, economic and social factors (Homer-Dixon 1999: 178). For instance, the discovery of new mineral resources in Africa is already attracting old and new global powers to the region, and there is a good prospect for increased revenues. If corruption and bad governance are not addressed, horizontal inequality and mismanagement of resources, including lack of fairness and justice in allocating wealth and other opportunities, will lead to new civil wars in Africa. Another factor promoting the regional character of African conflict is the social and economic networks built on informal trading and occupational and religious activities across many states dating back to the precolonial period (Adetula 2003). Trade and commercial networks have always been part of the social processes in West Africa, where Hausa traders and Fulani nomads are spread across many countries in West and Central Africa, just as the Masai are in East Africa and the Horn. The historical links have been replaced or transformed into contemporary transnational networks. In recent times, new migrant and trading networks and religious movements with complex organisational structures and institutions have emerged in the sub-region.

Since the end of the Cold War the world has witnessed an upsurge in transnational processes, including the rise of global social movements. As scholars shifted from state-centric analysis, the activities of non-state actors began to attract interest in academic as well as policy circles. This perspective now includes a rich intellectual discourse on transnational processes and their implications for national, regional and global peace and security . In this perspective, violent conflicts in parts of Africa are related to transnational processes such as the conflicts between pastoralists and farmers in West, East and Central Africa. There are also covert and illegal networks and transnational "dark networks" used for criminal or immoral ends such as child trafficking, prostitution, the illegal arms trade, illicit drug trading, currency trafficking, etc. many of which are a serious threat to peace and security.

Violent ethnic and religious conflicts now occur in the context of transnational relations in Africa, as in the case of the Tuareg rebels in the Sahel and the al-Shabaab movement in East Africa. Human trafficking, child slavery and other cross-border crimes are on the increase throughout Africa, in addition to mineral resource-driven conflicts. In recent times, West Africa has featured prominently in reported cocaine seizures by the US Drug Enforcement Administration. According to Stephen Ellis (2009: 173): "Not only is West Africa conveniently situated for trade between South America and Europe, but … it has a political and social environment … generally suitable for the drug trade. Smuggling is widely tolerated, law enforcement is fitful and inefficient, and politicians are easily bribed or even involved in the drug trade themselves." There is no doubt there are risks and threats to peace and security in Africa associated directly or indirectly with contemporary globalisation processes. In the next section, the principle and practice of collective security is discussed with a focus on its adaptation within the African integration system.

Also, there are new religious movements whose activities and influence are spread across the continent through modern information technology, including the internet. These modern means of communication have meant that the state loses absolute power over its territories. . It is now possible to see cultural and religious loyalty becoming stronger than national loyalty and becoming a serious concern for the state. Transnational religious movements are most visible in West Africa. Notably, some Nigeria-based Christian churches, such as Deeper Life Bible Ministries, Living Faith Church (Winners Chapel) and Redeemed Christian Church of God have branches across the sub-region. Similarly, the Niassenes Islamic Brotherhood and Celestial Church of Christ (CCC) have their foundation in Senegal and Benin respectively, but have pronounced transnational characteristics in West Africa. For example, the membership of the Niassenes Islamic brotherhood in Nigeria exceeds the entire population of Senegal. Meanwhile, CCC, especially under the late Pastor S.B.J Oschoffa, has become one of the most popular charismatic religious groupings in West Africa, with members throughout West Africa but concentrated in Benin, Nigeria, Togo and Côte d'Ivoire.

The complex and multiple linkages in African conflicts help to explain their intractability. Mali is a recent example of how conflict in one place can spread through the dispersal of fighters and arms. The flow of armed men and resources from Libya into northern Mali transformed the Tuareg campaign into a massive separatist movement. This insurgency by Islamist groups is seen in many West African circles as a threat to the entire sub-region. For instance, there is concern that the Malian conflict will spill over into Nigeria, where the Jama'atu Ahlis Sunna Lidda'awati wal-Jihad Islamist movement (popularly known as Boko Haram) is a serious national security risk. In 2012, President Deby of Chad expressed his concern that Boko Haram could destabilise the whole Lake Chad basin. He called on countries adjoining northern Nigeria to institute a joint military force to tackle the militants. It should be recalled that in 2013, when Chad faced a similar situation, it sent troops to support France to drive al-Qaeda allies out of northern Mali.

Similarly, in Central Africa the M23 movement in the DRC was reported to be enjoying the support of Rwanda and Uganda. Although both countries deny complicity in the conflict, this report has been a source of tension in the sub-region. In the same manner, Chad and Cameroun are threatened by the spill-over effects of the ongoing conflicts in the CAR. The Muslim Seleka movement that toppled the president of the CAR in March 2013 disintegrated shortly after reprisal attacks by Christian defence groups. Since 2012, Chadian troops have been in the CAR, first in the eastern part of the country and later in the capital, to help stabilise the country. The regional dimension of the conflict in Somalia is further complicated by the fact that Somalis are spread across five countries in the Horn, namely Kenya, Somali Republic, Djibouti, Eritrea and Ethiopia.

Globalisation has significantly changed the character and intensity of armed conflict in Africa. While globalisation is not new, its current wave entails increased mobility of financial capital as well as new kinds of migration, which in turn have created unprecedented tensions at several levels. Also, due to the benefits of advanced communication technologies, "major engines of globalisation" have penetrated national frontiers and created transnational identities that challenge national solidarity. It is possible to argue that globalisation is the primary cause of most of the new wars on the continent. It has brought new challenges to

Table I. Selected Major Armed Conflicts in Africa (January 2014)

Country	Characteristics	Status
CAR	Armed conflict started in December 2012 and escalated into large-scale sectarian violence. Within a few weeks of the outbreak more than 500 deaths were recorded, with many people displaced.	Live conflict
DRC	Despite the declaration of an end to insurgency in 2013, there has been general tension in the country, and the regrouping of the M23 is seen as new threat to security. Deaths from conflict were estimated to be 900,000 to 5.4m (Butty 2010)	Live conflict
Libya	Since Muammar Gaddafi's overthrow in 2011 there has been violence involving various militias and the new state security forces. The number of deaths in 2011 is still disputed, but it is estimated to be about 25,000.	Live conflict
Mali	Several insurgencies in northern Mali. On 22 March 2012, there was a coup that was followed by several destabilising events that attracted international responses. A 2013 peace deal between the government and Tuareg rebels was set aside by the rebels and fighting continues. Over 3,000 deaths have been reported in the media.	Live conflict
Nigeria	Insurgencies in Niger Delta by organised militant youths such as the Movement for Emancipation of the Niger Delta (MEND), and also the activities of two major Islamist groups in northern Nigeria, Boko Haram and Jamā'atu Anṣāril Muslimīna fī Bilādis Sūdān (also known as Ansaru). About 20,000 deaths reported in internal conflicts in Nigeria.	Live Conflict
Somalia	The country is largely controlled by feuding warlords with a very weak central government in Mogadishu.	Live conflict
South Sudan	Violence among various ethnicities continued throughout South Sudan's transition to independence in 2011 and has escalated since December 2013, especially between the Nuer and Dinka ethnicities. At least 1,000 people have been reported killed, and over 800 other people were injured in December 2013.	Live conflict
Sudan	Ruthless ethnic cleansing the Darfur region, leaving 1.5m homeless, 50,000 dead and over 200,000 in refugee camps in neighbouring countries.	Live conflict

governance and the management of public goods nationally and globally, and, in response, states are under pressure to adapt their relationships with other forces and agencies. The adoption of neoliberal economic policies and programmes in many countries, for instance, not only deregulated the economy, it "signed away" the power of the nation-state to regulate and enact policy to international bodies such as the International Monetary Fund (IMF) and World Bank. Pressures exerted by the latter on the political economy of countries in the global South continue to create social tensions. In 2011 there were Arab Spring revolts in Tunisia, Egypt, and Libya. For instance, in Nigeria the one-week nation-wide protest in January 2012 against the withdrawal of petroleum subsidies was illustrative of market-driven social conflicts. The lack of capacity by the state to effectively mediate and resolve social conflicts in many African countries experimenting with liberal political and economic reform programmes has resulted in further escalation of violent conflicts.

The idea of collective security is rooted in concerns about how to prevent the abuse of power by states and promote peace and security in the international system. The classic work by Innis Claude on the development of international organisations in the 20th century is highly relevant. His study reveals the evident preoccupation with the idea of collective security and the "antiwar orientations" that informed efforts to construct international organisations (1971: 216). Thus, the League of Nations was established with the expectation that it would transcend politics in its operations, and that its establishment would mark the birth of a new world order. David Mitrany is acknowledged as the father of functionalism in international relations. With his early work on *A Working Peace System* (1943) he pioneered modern integrative theory. His central argument is that international cooperation is the best way to soften antagonisms in the international environment. He thus made a strong case in support of functional cooperation as the solution to the global peace problem: "the problem of our time is not how to keep nations peacefully apart but how to bring them actively together" (1966: 28). Thus he recommended the establishment of functional agencies to foster international cooperation, mainly in the technical and economic sectors. He argued this approach could eventually enmesh national governments in a dense network of interlocking cooperative ventures.

In 1945 the United Nations was formed around the concept of collective security. It replaced the League of Nations, which had been unable to prevent the outbreak of the Second World War. During the discussions preceding the formation of the UN, there was debate about whether the new security system should be oriented towards regionalism, as advocated by Moscow and London, or towards universalism, as Washington favoured. A proposal was made by the Great Powers to the San Francisco Conference in June 1945 to create an international collective security organisation. However, changes were made to allow regional organisations to manage conflicts between their members. This was prompted by three considerations: (i) a regional approach to interstate conflicts held more promise of eliciting collaboration; (ii) global rivalries and divisions might inhibit the UN in dealing with some types of conflicts; and (iii) some countries were not too enthusiastic about Great Power intervention in their regions (Zacher 1979: 2). Whatever the strength of these concerns, they provided the justification for the UN provisions in Articles 51–54.

According to Robert Lieber (1973), "peaceful change would come not through a shift of national boundaries but by means of action taken across them."(1973: 42). Some states would not readily compromise their sovereignty except to transfer executive authority for specific ends. Functional cooperation in areas of need therefore seemed the only workable alternative for promoting world peace. The neo-functionalists improved on the functionalist strategy based essentially on European integration. Ernst Haas, Leon Lindberg, Phillip Schmitter and Stuart Scheingold are quite illuminating in this regard. Some neo-functionalists have likened behaviour in a regional setting to that in modern pluralist nation-states motivated by self-interest, and conclude that there is a continuum between economic integration and political union made possible through automatic politicisation. They argued that actors become involved in an incremental process of decision-making, beginning with economic and social matters (welfare maximisation) and gradually moving to the political sphere. They also prescribed "supranational agency" as a condition for "effective problem-solving," which slowly expands so as "to progressively undermine the independence of the nation-states." (Lindberg and Scheingold 1970: 6). That political actors will "shift their loyalties, expectations and political activities toward a new centre, whose institutions possess on demand jurisdiction over the pre-existing national states" is a central assumption of the neo-functionalists (Haas 2004: 16).

As a theory of regional integration, neo-functionalism identifies three causal factors that interact. These are: (i) growing economic interdependence between nations; (ii) organisational capacity to resolve disputes and build international legal regimes; and (iii) supranational market rules that replace national regulatory regimes (Haas 1961; Sandholtz and Sweet 1997). There is a sense in which early neo-functionalist theory reflects the idealist assumption that nation-states would pursue welfare objectives through their commitment to political and market integration at a higher, supranational level. In his work, *The Uniting of Europe: Political, Social, and Economic Forces, 1950–1957*, Haas pointed to three mechanisms as the driving forces behind regional integration. These were positive spill-over, the transfer of domestic allegiances and technocratic automaticity (Haas 2004).

There are two fundamental fallacies in functionalist/neo-functionalist assumptions: the separability of *Grosspolitik* from welfare issues and the potential of international organisations. That peace can be automatically achieved through economic and social internationalisation raises the question of whether states can be made to join in a functional sector before settling their outstanding political and security issues. Apart from the "priority fallacy," there is also the problem of ultimate transfer of loyalty and sovereignty from states to international organisations. One key justification for such transfer of loyalty is the assumption that supranational agencies are better equipped to promote the interests of people and states. However, judging by the operation of functionally specific international agencies, few have moved far in the direction of the neo-functionalist assumption that people are willing and capable of pressing their governments to transfer powers to international bodies (Deutsch 1978: 210).

The OAU was established in 1963 as the collective security apparatus for Africa. UN Articles 51–54 justified its creation. In 2002, the AU replaced the OAU. Between the OAU and the UN Economic Commission for Africa (UNECA), many sub-regional integration schemes were "midwifed," initially for economic purposes. The OAU's regional approach found easy accommodation within the assumptions of the idealist school. However, the OAU, besides lacking political courage, lacked the institutional capacity to manage conflicts. Despite the provisions in its charter that it should settle African disputes and conflicts, its performance in this area was hardly impressive. The first Pan-African peacekeeping mission took place in Shaba province in the DRC (Zaire) in 1978–79. It was after this that the OAU undertook a peace operation in Chad in 1979–82 (Williams 2006: 353). Yet by the end of the Cold War, the OAU had still not emerged as a regional organisation with sufficient clout. This, coupled with other developments in international relations, prompted a rethinking of peace and development in Africa, and the associated role of regional organisations.

Similarly, the UN had little success in managing conflicts. Its inability to raise a UN enforcement force in accordance with Chapter VII of the UN Charter was a major limitation. The effects of the Cold War, as well as power politics among powerful states, affected the UN's capacity to manage conflicts, including the deployment of peacekeeping operations. Throughout the Cold War, the world's hegemonic powers in effect determined the direction of conflicts and co-operation in the international system. The US was about the largest contributor to UN peacekeeping operations, and its interests were never to be compromised. For instance, following the brutal killing of American soldiers in Somalia, the US and other Western countries scaled back their support for UN peacekeeping operations in Africa, thus undermining the capacity of the UN to mount such operations. It can be said that UN peacekeeping operations during that period were "dramatic failures." In this regard it is important to mention the dismal performance of the UN peacekeeping mission in Somalia and the failure of the mission to halt the 1994 genocide in Rwanda.

These and related developments informed the quest to improve UN peacekeeping operations, beginning with Boutros Ghali's 1992 Agenda for Peace and the Brahimi-led Panel on United Nations Peace Keeping Operations (2000). The latter, in its report, acknowledged the importance of regional and sub-regional organisations in establishing and maintaining peace and security. The UN Security Council (UNSC) later adopted the recommendation that regional organisations assume primary responsibility for managing conflicts in their neighbourhood. In some respects, this arrangement harmonises with the new idea of "African solutions to African problems" that followed the West's declining inclination to support UN peacekeeping operations in Africa and the growing desire of Africans to be more involved in their own affairs, including conflict management and resolution on the continent.

As noted, participation by regional organisations in establishing and maintaining peace and security is not a recent development. Chapter VIII of the UN Charter provides for "regional arrangements or agencies dealing with such matters relating to the maintenance of international peace and security." Such arrangements and agencies are to complement the UNSC, which has primary responsibility for international peace and security, and the UN Charter states in Article 53 that "no enforcement action shall be taken under regional arrangements or by regional agencies without the authorization of the Security Council, with the exception of measures against an enemy state". Also, regional arrangements and agencies are to have adequate capacity to undertake such action, "either on the initiative of the states concerned or by reference from the Security Council." However, the Nigerian-led ECOMOG intervention in Liberia was launched without UNSC authorisation. The seeming unwillingness of powerful states to maintain world peace imposed new responsibilities on regional actors like Nigeria, whose claim that Liberia would otherwise experience a total breakdown of law and order that could threaten regional peace and security could not be dismissed.

The case of the AU's initial intervention in the Darfur crisis was different. The AU intervened without adequate enforcement capabilities. The African Standby Force was not yet established and logistics were in short supply when the UNSC encouraged the AU to embark on its first African peace mission, the African Mission in Sudan (AMIS).

Arguably these developments reflected the new realities of the post-Cold War international system. On one hand, they suggest the resurgence of idealism in the management of inter-state relations whereby international relations are increasingly defined not in terms of old power politics but in anticipation of a system of collective security that "would require the great powers to renounce both the use of force in disputes among themselves and unilateral action in regional conflicts" (McNamara 1992: 100). On the other, one is not fully optimistic that the idealistic multipolar international system with new responsibilities and obligations for states and international organisations is realisable. Recent developments demonstrate that post-Cold War international violence cannot be managed exclusively on the basis of idealist expectations. The Gulf War and crises in Somalia, Haiti, Yugoslavia, Bosnia, Afghanistan, Iraq, Côte d'Ivoire, Libya and most recently Syria best illustrate the illusion of the new idealism.

Developments since the Cold War have offered increased opportunities for "finding regional solutions" (Wallensteen 2012: 4). In Europe, Germany and the UK got serious about promoting security in Europe using regional organisations and other alliances. In Asia, Japan and China have assumed the mantle of regional actors. In Africa, regional approaches to development, conflict prevention and management and promoting good governance are becoming popular among state and non-state actors. The broadening of the role of African regional organisations to include peacebuilding and conflict management adds weight to the efficacy of regional integration. Regionalist approaches to development and security rely on the leadership of regional hegemons and pivotal states to be effective. The modern world system is filled with instances of the positive and negative uses of hegemonic power. Hegemonic states should normally be large and capable of projecting power beyond their own borders in a disinterested way. While this may not be wholly true of France, the UK and US, which cannot be said to have intervened in postcolonial Africa without biases and interests, it is plausible that there are elements of altruism in the hegemonic roles of some core states in Africa, notably Nigeria and South Africa, around which several initiatives to promote regional peace and security were built.

These two countries have been playing the role of regional hegemons in Africa, serving as hubs for most new regional initiatives. Both have potential and actual capabilities as regional powers, in terms of political and socioeconomic vision, aspirations to leadership, political legitimacy, military capability, resource endowment and political willingness to implement those visions. Both have invested much in the promotion of regional security and good governance in Africa. South Africa accounts for about one-third of Africa's economic strength and has adequate military capacity to play the role of regional hegemon. Similarly, Nigeria is the wealthiest state in West Africa with by far the largest military force in the sub-region. While neither may readily be considered a regional hegemon in the strict sense of the word, both have been operationalising their visions of hegemonic power in their respective sub-regions, and also continentally in cooperation with other partners.

This role has been to the benefit of Africa. For example, Nigeria in the 1970s led the 46 member African, Caribbean, and Pacific group of countries (ACP) in the negotiations with the European Community that resulted in the Lomé Convention on 28 February 1975. This initiative helped ACP states evolve an identity of their own through the promotion of regional cooperation among themselves (Sanu and Adetula 1989: 28). It was in the same period that Nigeria took the lead by floating the idea of broad West African integration, an initiative that culminated in the establishment of ECOWAS in June 1975, just months after the Lomé Convention. Nigeria also initiated the first sub-regional intervention to ensure peace in a crisis in Africa. Also, Nigeria and post-apartheid South Africa championed the birth of the AU and inauguration of NEPAD. This high level commitment to pan-African integration by these two countries and a number of others like Algeria, Egypt, Libya and Tunisia, has encouraged the involvement of regional organisations in promoting peace and security on the continent.

The world today is experiencing a reawakening of supranationalism. The EU is commendable in balancing "inter-governmentalism" and "supranationalism." This hybrid model is fast gaining prominence in the operations of most international and regional organisations, with nation-states pushing for greater cooperation among themselves. There is now broader and deeper integration among nation-states in various regions of the world, and also non-states and sub-national actors are increasingly relevant in areas previously the domain of the nation-state, including peace and security. African states that hitherto "held on to idea of nation-state and national sovereignty appear to be on the path towards rejecting both ... [With] the resurgence of 'African consciousness' they are demonstrating renewed commitment to regional and continental institutions through numerous treaties in pursuit of regional integration" (Oppong 2011: 1). Arguably the transformation of the OAU into the AU benefited from the paradigm shift that favours the coexistence of supranationalism and inter-governmentalism. The incorporation of supranationality into the Treaty Establishing the African Economic Community came first, and it encouraged other integrative arrangements that subscribed to the principle and practice of supranationalism. The establishment of the AU, and some follow-up activities, including the transformation of the AU Commission into the African Authority, have further institutionalised African supranationalism. These developments have a significant impact on the roles of Africa's regional organisations in managing African conflicts.

During the struggle for African political independence, continental unity and regional cooperation was acknowledged as a strategy for combating dependence and underdevelopment. In postcolonial Africa, regional cooperation is motivated by broad economic, social and political interests, and the need for greater international bargaining power. Today, it is rare to find an African country uninterested in at least one regional cooperation scheme on the continent. Over the past five decades, Africa has experimented with more than 200 regional intergovernmental organisations, most of them claiming to promote regional cooperation (See Table II). The practical results, however, have been disappointing. Yet African governments have continued to promote regional cooperation as a strategy for self-reliance and development.

The membership of African governments in regional economic integration schemes is a *sine qua non* for development. The argument is that integration of the continent's economies will result in large markets capable of stimulating industrialisation and moving Africa towards sustainable development. However, these outcomes have eluded the continent partly because of instability and the many instances of violent conflict. Peace and security promote regional integration, and vice versa. For example, the AMU, which would have brought the economies of Morocco, Algeria, Tunisia and Mauritania closer together never took-off because three of the core states sharply disagreed over Western Sahara: Morocco's claims to the former Spanish colony were contested by Algeria and Mauritania, which supported autonomy for the territory.

Since the end of the Cold War, it has become abundantly clear that Africa must rely less on the generosity of the global North for both development processes and conflict management. The volume of development assistance to the global South has declined significantly, making the pursuit of Africa's self-reliance ever more imperative. Also, since Operation Restore Hope in Somalia in 1992, Western countries have become less enthusiastic about getting involved in Africa's conflicts. Significantly, Africa has acknowledged this reality and adjusted accordingly, as evidenced by the establishment of the OAU Mechanism for Conflict Prevention, Management and Resolution in 1993. The subsequent inauguration of NEPAD and establishment of the AU were two related initiatives deeply rooted in the philosophy of self-reliance. NEPAD, Africa's latest plan for economic development, is based on the New African Initiative (NAI), a merger of the Millennium Partnership for the African Recovery Programme (MAP) and the Omega Plan. It has been described as "Africa's strategy for achieving sustainable development in the 21st century" (Anyang' Nyong'o et al. 2002: vi). Regional and sub-regional approaches to development are a key element in accomplishing many of the expected results.

Table II. Major Regional Integration Arrangements in Africa

Grouping	Est. Year	Member States
African Union (AU). Its predecessor, the OAU, had existed in parallel with the African Economic Community (AEC) that was established in 1991. In 2001 NEPAD was formed and it later became part of the AU structures.	2000	Fifty-four independent African countries acceded as members of the AU. However, Morocco left the OAU in 1984. Also, CAR was suspended in March 2013, and Egypt in July 2013
Arab Maghreb Union (AMU) is based on a trade agreement to promote economic cooperation and political unity among Arab countries of the Maghreb.	1989	Algeria, Libya, Mauritania, Morocco and Tunisia.
Communauté Économique et Monétaire de l'Afrique Centrale (CEMAC) or Central African Economic and Monetary Community	1999	Gabon, Cameroon, CAR, Chad, Republic of Congo and Equatorial Guinea
East Africa Community (EAC) II. EAC I was established in 1967. It later became moribund. It was revived in 1999.	1999	Burundi, Kenya, Rwanda, Tanzania and Uganda. In 2010 it expanded to include the members of SADC and COMESA.
Southern African Customs Union (SACU)	1910	Botswana, Lesotho, Namibia, South Africa and Swaziland.
Mano River Union (MRU)	1973	Liberia, Sierra Leone and Guinea.
West African Economic and Monetary Union (WAMU). It replaced West African Economic Community (CEAO) that was formed in 1973.	1994	Benin, Burkina Faso, Côte d'Ivoire, Mali, Mauritania, Niger, Senegal
Economic Community of West African States (ECOWAS)	1975	Benin, Burkina Faso, Cape Verde, Côte d'Ivoire, The Gambia, Ghana, Guinea, Guinea-Bissau, Liberia, Mali, Mauritania (until 1999), Niger, Nigeria, Senegal, Sierra Leone, Togo
Economic Community of the Great Lakes countries (CEPGL)	1976	Burundi, Rwanda, DRC, Rwanda
Intergovernmental Authority on Development (IGAD) replaced IGADD that was formed in1986	1996	Djibouti, Eritrea, Ethiopia, Kenya, Somalia, Sudan and Uganda
Southern African Development Community (SADC) was established in August 1992 in Windhoek, Namibia, to replace the Southern African Development Coordination Conference (SADCC).	1992	Angola, Botswana, DRC, Lesotho, Malawi, Mauritius, Mozambique, Namibia, Seychelles, South Africa, Swaziland, Tanzania, Zambia and Zimbabwe.
Community of Sahel-Saharan States (CEN-SAD)	1998	Burkina Faso, Chad, Libya, Mali, Niger, Sudan, CAR, Eritrea, Djibouti, Gambia, Senegal, Egypt, Morocco, Nigeria, Somalia, Tunisia, Benin, Togo. Côte d'Ivoire, Guinea-Bissau, Liberia, Ghana, Sierra Leone, Comoros, Guinea, Kenya, Mauritania, São Tomé and Príncipe
Economic Community of Central African States (ECCAS)	1984	Angola, Burundi, Cameroon, CAR, Chad, DRC, Equatorial Guinea, Gabon, Rwanda, and São Tomé and Príncipe
Common Market for Eastern and Southern Africa (COMESA). It replaced the PTA	1994	Originally had 16 members but now has 19. Membership has undergone many changes. In 2008 COMESA agreed to an expanded free-trade zone including members of EAC and SADC. Membership at different times included Burundi, Comoros, DRC, Djibouti, Eritrea, Ethiopia, Kenya, Madagascar, Malawi, Mauritius, Rwanda, Sudan, Swaziland, Uganda, Zambia, Zimbabwe, Angola, Lesotho, Mozambique, Namibia, Tanzania, Egypt, Seychelles and Libya.

By the late 1970s, it had become evident that the OAU Charter needed amendment to enable the organisation to cope better with the challenges and realities of a changing world. Consequently, in 1979 a committee was established to review the Charter, but was unable to formulate substantial amendments. However, for the OAU to remain relevant, the Charter was "amended" and augmented essentially through ad hoc decisions of the summit, including the Cairo Declaration Establishing the Mechanism for Conflict Prevention, Management and Resolution. Even so, it was increasingly necessary for the OAU to work towards greater efficiency. There was an urgent need to integrate the political activities of the OAU with the provisions of the AEC treaty on economic and development issues to avoid duplication. Thus on 9 September 1999, the extraordinary OAU summit in Sirte, Libya called for the establishment of the AU in conformity with the ultimate objectives of the OAU Charter and the provisions of the AEC treaty. The Consultative Act of the African Union was adopted during the Lomé Summit of the OAU on 11 July 2000. At the fifth extraordinary OAU/AEC summit held in Sirte, from 1–2 March 2001, a decision declaring the establishment of the AU based on the unanimous will of member states was adopted, and the AU came into being at the 2002 OAU Summit, held in South Africa.

The AU's objectives strengthen the founding principles of the OAU Charter, but are also more comprehensive: they acknowledge the multifaceted challenges confronting the continent, especially in the areas of peace and security, socio-economic development and integration. The AU is intended to accelerate political and socioeconomic integration; promote common Africa positions; promote democratic institutions, popular participation and good governance; protect human rights; promote sustainable development and the integration of African economies; eradicate preventable diseases and promote good health. President Museveni of Uganda justified the AU thus: "What we actually need is to amalgamate the present 53 states of Africa into either one African Union or, at least, seven or so more viable states: West African Union, Congo, the East African Union, the Southern African Union, the Horn of Africa Union, the Maghreb Union with Egypt and Sudan" (2001: 12).

The renewed commitment to Pan-Africanism and the inclination towards a federalist approach to regional integration has taken place in a global context characterised by the demise of the territorial state in international relations and a growing desire for deeper integration in Africa. Also, there is growing awareness in Africa of the effectiveness of regional integration and cooperative schemes in the prevention and management of conflicts and in circumventing the clause on non-interference in the internal affairs of African states that almost crippled the OAU. Of this clause, Nelson Mandela once said: "[African leaders] cannot abuse the concept of national sovereignty to deny the rest of the continent the right and duty to intervene, when, behind those boundaries, people are being slaughtered to protect tyranny" (1998: 2). Hutchful lends credence to Mandela's notion of "sovereignty as responsibility" by noting that the "defence of democracy and proper governance" is an appropriate ground for intervention in the internal affairs of other states (1998: 1). Indeed, the AU's establishment marked the beginnings of a qualitative change in African integration, one that seeks to promote Pan-African regional integration over pseudo-nationalist and state-centric notions of sovereignty.

The AU's Constitutive Act places a premium on the promotion of peace, security and stability in Africa (Article 3 (f)). Also enshrined in its principles are the peaceful resolution of conflicts; prohibition of the use of force or threats to use force; and, unlike the OAU, rights to intervene in the affairs of member states in "grave circumstances" related to war crimes, genocide and crimes against humanity (Articles 4 (c), (f) and (h)). The Act provides for several institutions to carry out the operations of the AU. These include the assembly, executive council, Pan-African Parliament, African Court of Justice, commission, committee of permanent representatives, specialised technical committee, and Economic Social and Cultural Council. Article 19 of the act provides for the AU's financial institutions, including the African Central Bank, African Monetary Fund and African Investment Bank. The AU has a number of special programmes to facilitate its vision and quicken the realisation of its goals. These are NEPAD, the African Peer Review Mechanism (APRM) and the Conference on Security Stability Development and Cooperation in Africa (CSSDCA).

Although the OAU Charter provided for the organisation to settle African disputes and conflicts, the OAU's performance in this area was hardly impressive. This, coupled with the dwindling interest of the global North in Africa's challenges and the apparent incapacitation of the UN as a result the politics of the UNSC (Annan 2013) necessitated a rethinking of the best approach to ensuring peace and security in Africa. The AU and regional economic communities (RECs) have been playing a larger peace and security role in Africa through their involvement in several regional collective security operations. While ECOWAS intervention in Liberia marked the starting point for RECs, the AU's initiation was in the Burundi peace operations in 1994.

Continental-level Initiatives

The main AU mechanism for promoting peace and security is the African Peace and Security Architecture (APSA). Its key elements include the Peace and Security Council (PSC), a Continental Early Warning System (CEWS), the African Stand-by Force (ASF), the Panel of the Wise (PoW) and the Peace Fund. APSA is designed to work with national and sub-regional actors as the main sources of capability in conflict management. It is designed to function in collaboration with RECs and regional mechanisms for its operationalisation. The inaugural AU summit in 2002 agreed to establish a PSC for preventing managing, and revolving conflicts in Africa. The July 2002 Durban Protocol described it as "a collective security and early-warning arrangement to facilitate timely and efficient response to conflict and crisis situations in Africa." Thus in principle the PSC has extensive powers to address virtually all threats to regional peace and security in Africa. In addition, the PSC can institute sanctions against governments that come to power through unconstitutional means; and monitor the promotion of democratic practices, good governance, the rule of law, protection of human rights and fundamental freedoms, respect for the sanctity of human life and international humanitarian law by member states. The PSC has also to "promote and develop a strong partnership for peace and security between the AU and the United Nations and its agencies, as well as with other relevant international organizations," and "develop policies and action required to ensure that any external initiative in … peace and security on the continent take place within the framework of the Union's objectives and priorities."

Since its establishment in 2004, the PSC has recorded some progress in building its capacity to enhance AU conflict resolution and mediation efforts. The PSC has so far held close to 300 meetings at various levels. Decisions taken covered a variety of conflicts and conflict-related issues, such as the armed violence in Sudan and Somalia; unconstitutional change in Guinea, Niger, Togo and Mauritania; global terrorism; small arms and light weapons; and children and women in armed conflicts. Although modelled on the UNSC, the PSC does not yet have similar powers and authority. Nonetheless, the PSC has sought to promote African security within a strategic partnership between AU and UN. There is already evidence of evolving AU-UN cooperation in the area of information sharing. This has contributed to the success of the African Union Mission in Somalia (AMISOM). However, such cooperation is less evident in the cases of Mali and the CAR. Both UN and AU still harbour suspicions of each other, which makes cooperation between them very difficult. Other problems confronting the PSC include its inadequate funding and lack of status in relation to sub-regional organisations. Also, the PSC faces the challenge of how to manage its relationship with the AU Commission, which tends to assume a de facto supervisory role of the PSC.

The ASF is a critical element of APSA and of the AU's peacekeeping capacity. One of the lessons learned from the Rwandan genocide was the need for an African stand-by force that would lessen dependence on the international community to maintain peace on the continent. Article 4 (d) of the Constitutive Act therefore provides for the establishment of "a common defence and security policy" for Africa. The ASF was established in 2003 with responsibility for observation, monitoring and other peace-support missions; intervention in a member state if necessary; preventive deployment; and peacebuilding, including post-conflict disarmament and demobilisation. It is not a standing army but it is designed to enable the AU to deploy troops swiftly to preserve peace and prevent or contain conflict. It has five multinational standby brigades, each hosted by one of the five African regions (North, South, East, West and Central). The five RECs – AMU, IGAD, ECCAS, ECOWAS and SADC – are closely associated with ASF operations.

To avoid complications in regions where not all countries belong to the same REC or where some countries belong to more than one, AU opted for ASF regional mechanisms. For example, AMU could not assume responsibility for a standby brigade because Egypt is part of AMU and Morocco is not an AU member. Thus, the North African Regional Capability (NARC) was formed as the regional mechanism for North Africa and NASBRIG as its standby brigade. Similarly, in East Africa, where Rwanda is not a member of IGAD, the Eastern Africa Standby Brigade Command was formed as the regional mechanism and EASBRIG the standby brigade. In West, Central and Southern Africa, where the RECs have broad membership, it was not difficult for them to upgrade their structures to establish a regional standby force to support the ASF. Thus, ECOWAS created a regional force, ECOBRIG, with the Nigerian military as its main component. While it has helped resolve various conflicts in the region, it was unable to respond promptly to the Malian crisis in 2012. The SADC stand-by force – SADCBRIG – was launched in 2007 but is still poorly equipped and lacks the capacity for effective intervention. The ECCAS regional force is known as Force Multinationale de l'Afrique Central (FOMAC). It, however, failed to stabilise the threatening situation in East Africa in early 2013. There were serious capacity gaps, which the deployment of 200 South African troops did little to address. ECCAS eventually asked South Africa to withdraw its troops after they suffered casualties.

The ASF has not been without major challenges. First, the shared AU-REC control of the stand-by forces has complicated matters and become a major frustration for the Union. Second, the line of authority to deploy the ASF as between the AU and RECs is unclear. Also, there is growing concern that a strong ASF may compete with the AU rather than complement it. The situation today is that the AU confronts the challenges associated with launching military operations that are executed by regional organisations. These problems become more daunting when the AU and regional bodies do not share common interests and objectives for peace operations. In such situations, the execution of AU mandates may be plagued by delays, poor logistics and inadequate human and material resources. Second, funding to operationalise the ASF remains a serious problem. Operationalisation of various components of APSA generally benefits from wide partner support. However, given the AU's poor resource profile compared to the RECs', the latter are more influential in the deployment of regional standby forces. Third, and closely related to the above, are the concerns about the viability of the ASF as a collection of regionally based brigade-level joint forces capable of responding quickly to peace and stability threats.

One can argue that coordination between the AU and the RECs/regional mechanisms has improved. For example, ASF and CEWS have clearly articulated roadmaps, and hence a structured basis for their operationalisation. Moreover, the appointment of the REC/regional mechanism liaison officers to the AU has improved communications between the two levels. Similarly, the deployment of the AU liaison officers to RECs/regional mechanisms has further boosted coordination. However, the other components of APSA (PSC, PoW and Peace Fund) remain largely uncoordinated. For example, there are no strong linkages between them and similar structures in the RECs/regional mechanisms. Because of this, processes and procedures rely on personal relationships between the AU chairperson and REC/regional mechanism chief executives. This has serious implications for effective coordination and for managing relationships.

Also, horizontal coordination among APSA components has not been impressive. For instance, the PSC has derived little benefit in its decision-making process from data, information and analyses from AU and REC early warning systems. Also, the interface between RECs/regional mechanisms has not shown significant progress despite overlapping membership in some of them. However, within the framework of the APSC there has been some inter-REC/regional mechanism coordination. For instance, COMESA, EAC and IGAD have produced a number of outcomes, including a joint conflict prevention management and resolution programme for East Africa on small arms and light weapons and on pastoralist conflicts and cross-border issues. Nonetheless, coordination among RECs/regional mechanisms remains a big challenge.

Notwithstanding these limitations, the AU has deployed a number of peace operations in Africa, including in Burundi (AMIB), Darfur (AMIS) and Somalia (AMISOM). Also, there have been other AU-led peace missions such as the electoral and security assistance mission to the Comoros (MAES) and the complementary "Operation Democracy" on the Comorian island of Anjouan. These were the first AU peace-enforcement missions. They were "two different types of interventions and represent two roles for the African Union in attempting to support peace and security on the Africa continent" (Svensson 2008: 7). Other recent interventions by the AU include the missions in Mali (AFISMA) and the CAR (MISCA), which are now part of a multilateral peacekeeping initiative. Each of these missions and operations had its own successes and challenges, which are already well documented and need not detain us. However, it suffices to say that they yielded useful lessons. For example, AMISOM was deployed in 2007. It is still the largest and most complex regional peacekeeping mission in Africa under a UN mandate. Recent Africa-led missions in Mali and CAR suggest that AMISOM may be a model under Chapter VII of the UN Charter on regional enforcement operations in Africa (Fahlén 2015 forthcoming). Other cases of AU involvement in peace missions have helped uncover the deficiencies in the existing peacekeeping architecture and mechanisms as well as the strengths and limitations of national, regional and global actors. For instance, coordination between the AU and UN was not always of the best. Poor AU-UN consultation on the situation in Libya complicated coordination of their positions, even though it was almost certain the West was out for regime change rather than the negotiated political settlement that the AU seemed to favour. When France decided to send soldiers into the CAR in November 2013, some thought it had done the right thing for the wrong reason. The case of Mali demonstrated the AU's poor state of preparedness and capacity gaps, leading perceptive observers to conclude that the organisation may be biting off more than it can chew.

As scholars of peace-building and practitioners in the field reflect on past and ongoing peace missions in Africa, the case of CAR deserves further examination. In CAR, the AU was at the mercy of France, which along with the UN and AU dispatched some 4,000 troops, but only after French Foreign Minister Laurent Fabius warned that the CAR was "on the verge of genocide." Because earlier AU advice that all efforts be coordinated to avert inter-communal pogroms in CAR was ignored by the international community, including France, it appeared that the latter was more concerned that the conflict in CAR not spill over into neighbouring Cameroon and DRC, where it has strategic political and economic interests. The characterisation of the crises of CAR as a genocide by the French eventually paid off. France obtained a UNSC resolution authorising its troops to use "all necessary measures." The mission was to hand over disarmed militias to the African-led International Support Mission in the Central African Republic (MISCA), which the UNSC charged with stabilising the country for 12 months.

The state of insecurity in Libya following the overthrow of Moammar Gadhafi demonstrated the dangers of misdiagnosing African conflicts and proffering wrong solutions. Also, the difference between the AU and UN over the Libyan crisis shows the deterioration in relations between the two. Feeling ignored in what they considered their own affairs, Africans are reiterating the slogan "African solutions to African problems." While the importance of the AU-UN relationship cannot be underestimated, the international community must acknowledge that there are issues particular to Africa that are important in any assessment of the AU's peace and security mandates. The workings of AU institutions and structures for ensuring peace and security are further reviewed below with a focus on constraints and limitations.

There are three sources of funding for the AU generally: ordinary budget funds, voluntary contributions from member states, and other sources, notably support from international donors and partners. Inadequate resources for AU institutions and structures remain a big challenge. The AU budget also faces arrears in contributions, estimated in 2010 to be about US$ 43 million. Political instability in some rich North African countries, notably Egypt and Libya, and the "cold" rivalry among certain powerful and influential member states seem to be diverting interest away from the AU, with implications for its finances. A significant proportion of the AU budget has been contributed in the past by rich and powerful countries, notably Algeria, Angola, Kenya, Nigeria and South Africa. Since becoming AU Commission chairperson in 2012, Nkosazana Dlamini-Zuma has pushed for a more self-sufficient AU to end the dependence on external funding. The projected AU budget for 2013 was US$ 278.2 million, more than half of which was expected to come from foreign sources. There were attempts at seeking new funding, including private-sector finance and taxes on extra-African imports and air travel. However, these have not been pursued systematically.

Operationalisation of APSA has been largely dependent on partner support. This has serious implications for sustainability, predictability and flexibility. Both the EU and G8 recognise the AU as important to African conflict resolution and have provided some support for its mechanisms. However, in coming years this support from the West may decrease, especially with the economic crisis in Europe. For example, France after its involvement in Mali and the CAR to restore peace is seemingly retreating from resolving the continent's conflicts, particularly in terms of financial contributions. It has already begun to advocate increased financial contributions by African countries for peace operations on the continent. Similarly, other Western countries are willing to endorse "African solutions for African problems," especially if it means using African troops in Africa's wars, and making African governments responsible for funding.

The relationship between the AU and RECs/regional mechanisms is supposed to be hierarchical but mutually reinforcing. In principle, the AU harmonises and coordinates REC/ regional mechanism peace and security activities, in part through the liaison officers mentioned above. However, in practice the principle of subsidiarity in the relationship between AU and the RECs /regional mechanisms is not very clear. For instance, some of the latter resist the AU Commission's role as implementing agency within APSA, especially on issues where they feel they have greater comparative strength.

A decade after its conception, the ASF is still far from being able to take charge of military interventions to maintain peace on the continent. In Libya, it was NATO that intervened militarily to prevent further deterioration of the crisis, while in Mali it was France that sent troops to prevent a total breakdown of order. Many African circles perceive that Africa was deliberately sidelined in Libya to pave the way for Western powers to overthrow Gadhafi. On the contrary, there was a serious threat of civilian massacres in Libya and the AU had no capacity to intervene effectively. Similarly, the failure of the AU to promptly intervene in Mali in early 2012 provided the opportunity for French intervention. The AU subsequently proposed a temporary mechanism – the African Capacity for Immediate Response to Crises (ACIRC) –based on a coalition of willing states and to be financed by AU member states on a voluntary basis. Interestingly, Chad, South Africa, Tanzania and Uganda pledged troops. Algeria, Angola, Ethiopia, Ghana, Niger and Sudan indicated a wish to be part of the mechanism in the future. However, the concern remains that ACIRC would face the same problems as the ASF.

The case of the CAR revealed the weaknesses of regional stand-by forces. In early 2013, the Central African Multinational Force was unable to stabilise the situation in the CAR, resulting in the deployment of the South African National Defence Force. The fact that ECCAS did not seek support from either ECOWAS or SADC raises troubling questions about capacity gaps as well regional politics that inhibit the effective performance of regional stand-by forces. Other constraints include lack of political will by African states to finance military operations outside their territories, inadequate military capability for effective peace enforcement and tensions among regional and sub-regional bodies over the leadership of peace operations.

Although the AU now has more responsibility for peace and security on the continent, the Constitutive Act is not specific as to the type of operations AU can undertake. Unlike the OAU, the AU has the "right to intervene in a member state pursuant to a decision of the PSC in respect of grave circumstances, namely war crimes, genocide, and crimes against humanity." It was in consideration of this major difference that Alpha Oumar Konare, the former AU Commission chair, described AU's emergence as a shift from "non-interference" in armed conflicts to "non-indifference" to member states' internal affairs. Scholars have also enthusiastically submitted that the AU's emergence and its adoption of the Constitutive Act suggest new approaches to the management of African conflicts. Abou Jeng highlights the provisions in Article 4 of the Constitutive Act on "non-indifference," "norms formulation" and "social integration and interdependence" as a significant paradigm shift in approaches to African peacebuilding and as the basis of the AU's peace and security framework (2012: 182). While one can interpret Article 4 as an African take on the principle of "Responsibility to Protect" and therefore as an innovation in AU peace and security architecture (Jeng 2012: 187), there are critical issues and areas that are omitted from the AU's normative and policy frameworks for conflict resolution. The slow AU response to popular uprisings in Tunisia, Libya and Egypt was not unconnected with the fact that such frameworks "offer no systematic and particular guidance on how to respond to popular democratic uprisings" (Dersso 2011: 36).

While APSA is a significant step forward as a regional mechanism for conflict resolution, it is important to ponder whether the AU is in a position to influence conflicts in terms of military capacity to conduct peace support operations and of promoting good governance and sustainable development in Africa. The AU may have moved far beyond the limitations of the OAU in terms of a vision to play a greater role in managing and resolving African conflicts, but its achievements to date do not match its ambitious declarations. While some AU challenges relate to capacity gaps, overall global influences also limit the AU. One area of concern in this regard is the relationships between the AU and other key global actors, especially the UN and EU.

Sub-regional Initiatives

The Economic Commission of Africa (ECA) was the earliest apostle of regional cooperation in Africa. It perceived internal markets in Africa as generally too small and therefore a constraint on industrialisation and development. Therefore economic cooperation and regional integration among African states was encouraged (Adetula 1992). In this context, African countries were expected to establish or strengthen multinational institutions to facilitate discussion and decisions on common policies and projects. However, the idea of an immediate regional market embracing all African countries was considered impractical. Thus, promoting sub-regional economic cooperation became an essential element of the ECA approach.

OAU-ECA collaboration, especially from the late 1970s, ushered in a new phase of regional cooperation in Africa. This phase witnessed the adoption of the Monrovia Colloquium (1979) and the Lagos Plan of Action (LPA) and the Final Act of Lagos (FAL) (1980). These processes culminated in the signing of the Abuja Treaty by the OAU heads of state and government establishing the African Economic Community (AEC) in 1991. All these initiatives acknowledged the need for the development of sub-regional economic groupings, usually in very colourful language. LPA envisaged the formation of an African common market by 2000, which was to be achieved in stages.

The aim of the AEC was to promote economic, social and cultural development as well as African economic integration in order to increase self-sufficiency and endogenous development and to create a framework for the mobilisation of materials and human resources. The Abuja Treaty provided for gradual coordination and harmonisation and progressive integration of the RECs in Africa. The implementation of the Abuja Treaty and establishment of AEC were to be achieved in a six-stage process lasting 34 years. The starting point was strengthening existing RECs and creating new ones as needed. Similarly, the AU has recognised eight RECs as official representative regional associations of African states.

Although these sub-regional schemes were set up primarily to promote economic interests, they have increasingly played a prominent role in recent peace processes in Burundi, Liberia, Sierra Leone, Guinea, Côte d'Ivoire, Zimbabwe, Mali and elsewhere. ECOWAS's intervention in the Liberian crisis was the first experiment in intervention by a sub-regional organisation. And even at that, it was more or else an ad hoc arrangement rather than a systematic peacebuilding undertaking, at least initially. The lessons learned from this early intervention by ECOWAS/ECOMOG in Liberia and other conflicts in West Africa helped in the building of a more formidable conflict-prevention and peacebuilding mechanism for and in West Africa.

After almost two decades, the treaty founding ECOWAS (1975) was found to be inadequate in the critical areas of political cooperation and regional peace and security. Other inadequacies include the weak binding effect of decisions by the authority and council, and ECOWAS's near absence of supranational power. Consequently, a committee of eminent persons to review the ECOWAS treaty was struck to consider the legislative powers of the authority of heads of state and government; the financing of community institutions; and the decision-making procedures of the authority and council of ministers. The committee identified four issues: institutional matters; political cooperation, regional peace and security; financing of regional integration efforts; and available options for cooperation and regional economic integration. The revised ECOWAS treaty was adopted by heads of state in July 1993. ECOWAS has since done very well in ensuring regional peace and security and in promoting democracy and good governance in the sub-region. Consequently, ECOWAS has earned a measure of international recognition. Since its intervention in Liberia, ECOWAS has intervened in Sierra Leone, Guinea-Bissau and Mali.

Under the revised treaty, a supranational security mechanism for conflict management and peacekeeping has progressed far more in West Africa. ECOWAS has scaled up its normative instruments and institutions to anticipate and confront peace and security challenges in the region, particularly with regard to conflicts and political governance. ECOWAS's security institutions comprise a mediation and security council, a defence and security commission and a council of elders. The first is made up of 10 members, and decisions are made by a majority of six or more members. Importantly, the ECOWAS security mechanism recognises the role of civil society in peace processes, particularly in the organisation's early warning system. In 2008, the ECOWAS Conflict Prevention Framework (ECPF) was adopted to guide the organisation's preventive diplomacy, which has further been strengthened by a Supplementary Protocol on Democracy and Good Governance, with its zero-tolerance for ascension to power through unconstitutional means. In Guinea-Bissau there is an ECOWAS peacekeeping mission, ECOMIB. ECOWAS is also implementing a multi-million dollar defence and security sector reform programme in the country as part of the efforts to restore peace and democracy there. The recent intervention by ECOWAS in Mali benefited from the efficiency of ECOWAS institutions as a result of ongoing reforms. The successful intervention by ECOWAS paved the way for the transformation of the African-led international support mission into a UN mission.

ECOWAS's success in conflict prevention and regional security is linked to the organisation's commitment to good governance and democratisation. To strengthen its regional security framework, in 2001 ECOWAS member states signed the original Protocol on Democracy and Good Governance (A/SP 1/12/01), supplementary to the Protocol establishing the Mechanism for Conflict Prevention, Management and Resolution, Peacekeeping and Security. The Protocol has 50 articles organised in three chapters, dealing with principles and modalities of implementation, sanctions and general and final provisions. It suffices to say that ECOWAS has worked closely with the AU and UN to restore order and legality in three member states, Guinea, Niger and Côte d'Ivoire. Similarly, ECOWAS's principles with respect to democracy and good governance guided its stand on presidential elections in Guinea, Niger, Benin and Nigeria. Concerns about the implications of Boko Haram for regional security in West Africa have been expressed by ECOWAS at different levels. The ECOWAS parliament has discussed the issue in one plenary session, noting that ECOWAS and other countries in the region were already finding ways to assist Nigeria. SADC has adopted a very similar model of regional collective security. Since the end of the apartheid era, SADC has undergone radical realignment, with South Africa becoming its de facto leader rather than its primary target. The 1992 treaty states that the consolidation, defence and maintenance of democracy, peace, security and stability are main objectives of the organisation. As with Nigeria and ECOWAS/ECOMOG, South Africa's involvement has contributed to the effectiveness of SADC's security and economic functions. SADC's conflict management strategy is based on the mandate of the Organ on Politics, Defence and Security Cooperation (OPDS), which is managed on a Troika basis, the Strategic Indicative Plan for the Organ (SIPO), SADC Protocol on Politics, Defence and Security Cooperation and the relevant UN and AU protocols. The OPDS is central to promoting peace and security in the SADC region. Along with other SADC institutions and structures, they are required to prevent, manage and resolve "inter and intra state conflicts, by peaceful means employing ... preventive diplomacy, negotiations, conciliation, and mediation." However, the SADC Protocol stresses strict respect for sovereignty, territorial integrity and non-aggression, while SIPO refers to mediation as a strategic activity not open to international partner funding. Predictably, these restrictions have implications for SADC's conflict-management performance, as in the cases of Zimbabwe and

Madagascar. OPDS was established in 1996 in the expectation that it would become the institutional framework within which SADC countries would co-ordinate their political, defence and security policies and activities. However, disagreement among members over the interpretation of certain sections of the charter has inhibited OPDS operations. Yet SADC has recorded some success in political mediation in the Comoros, Madagascar, Zimbabwe, Lesotho and the DRC. In the election-related conflicts in Madagascar and Zimbabwe, SADC mediation was guided by its Principles and Guidelines Governing Democratic Elections. The organisation is set to establish a mediation unit to enhance its mediation, conflict prevention and preventive diplomacy capacity.

However, the dream of a regional security community is still far from being realised in the SADC region. Several issues make cooperation among member states more difficult. One is the border dispute between Malawi and Tanzania. Article 9 of the SADC treaty empowers the SADC tribunal to adjudicate inter-state disputes. The tribunal is, however, suspended, and in its absence a media-tion process was instituted through the forum of former African heads of state and government, whose performance has not been very impressive. These poor performance indicators have not inspired much confidence in SADC's ability to ensure peace and stability in Southern Africa. SADC has been seen as biased in favour of Zimbabwe, following its endorsement of elections there as credible and peaceful. Also, SADC faces other constraints, including the absence of an ef-fective regional early warning system; poor political will and courage; weakness of especially the OPDS secretariat, which is subordinate to the Summit of the Heads of State and Government of SADC and cannot control member states; and lack of strong finances for mediation efforts. Also, while the SADC standby force is adequate for military operations, it lacks the capacity to manage human-itarian crises. Similarly, it has no comprehensive post-conflict reconstruction programme, which is necessary for sustainable peace in the region.

The Horn of Africa is bedevilled by serious inter- and intra-state conflicts. All the countries of IGAD have had significant internal security problems. For ex-ample, Sudan was engulfed by conflict for more than three decades. The newly independent South Sudan is almost torn apart by inter-ethnic conflicts. There are also border conflicts, pastoralist conflicts, piracy and terrorism. IGAD has begun to assert itself in the resolution of sub-regional conflicts in the Horn. Formed in 1986 and initially known as Inter-governmental Authority on Drought and Development, IGAD's primary task is coordinating regional re-source issues. Its membership now consists of Djibouti, Eritrea, Ethiopia, Kenya, Sudan and Uganda. In March 1996, the organisation's charter was amended to cover political and economic issues, including conflict resolution. With respect to the latter, periodic IGAD summits have served as forums for heads of state to discuss conflict and other issues. For example, at the 1986 IGAD summit the leaders of Ethiopia and Somalia were able to initiate talks that eventually led to détente and the demilitarisation of their borders (Deng 1996: 137). Because of perceived threats from conflicts in Somalia and Sudan, security issues received prompt attention from IGAD, especially in the early 1990s. Although its efforts were not successful, IGAD mediated in the civil war in Sudan in September 1993 and made a little headway in 1994. IGAD resumed its role in 1997, but not much was accomplished. Recently, IGAD pressured the two armed factions in South Sudan to begin talks on the peaceful resolution of violent conflict.

With pressure from the international community, IGAD has made peace and security a priority. IGAD executes its mandate on preventing, managing and resolving inter- and intra- state conflicts through political dialogue, a conflict early warning system (CEWARN) and cooperation with the AU. In 2006, IGAD proposed a peace-support mission to Somalia (IGASOM) charged with protecting Somali transitional federal institutions and creating a conducive atmosphere for the political process. The proposal was endorsed by the PSC. UNSC authorised IGAD and AU member states to establish a protection and training mission in Somalia without an enforcement mandate for six months (Fahlén 2015). The mission, however, never took place owing to controversy over the composition of the proposed force and also acute shortages of technical capacity and the material resources required for a mission of that scope (Fahlén 2015). Also, member states were over-sensitive about the issue of sovereignty and internal affairs, which, in addition to the unhealthy rivalry among them, ruled out the achievement of a broad-based consensus. For instance, there is the age-old border-conflict between Ethiopia and Eritrea. The latter suspended its membership in IGAD in order to avoid participating in military intervention in Somalia. Neither Sudan nor Ethiopia has the actual or potential attributes of a core state capable of assuming leadership of IGAD. Both countries face overwhelming domestic challenges. Also, while CEWARN is functioning, its limited coverage and lack of capacity to monitor conflict indicators across the sub-region is a major limitation. Closely related to this is the lack of enforcement of IGAD resolutions against member states, especially when conflict breaks out or in humanitarian emergencies (Hull et al. 2011: 9). In addition, IGAD faces a lack of funds. No member state is rich enough to provide support in the way that Nigeria supported ECOMOG operations in Liberia and Sierra Leone. Hence, the accomplishments of IGAD have remained quite modest compared with those of ECOWAS or even SADC.

Apart from ECOWAS, SADC and IGAD, there are a handful of lesser-known sub-regional initiatives on conflict prevention and management in Africa. These include ECCAS, AMU and the little-known Community of Sahelian-Saharan States that once mooted the creation of an intervention force to help settle the border dispute between Eritrea and Ethiopia. Interestingly, the revived EAC is giving due consideration to regional security and peace. In June 1998, three member states – Kenya, Tanzania and Uganda –together with the US undertook their first joint peacekeeping exercise.

In Central Africa, ECCAS, under the aegis of the AU and with EU support, is promoting political and security cooperation in the sub-region. Although its members have signed treaties and protocols such as the Protocol Establishing the Peace and Security Council for Central Africa, ECCAS still has no comprehensive policy framework for ensuring regional peace and security. However, it has been commended for brokering the January 2013 Libreville Peace Agreement. Also, at a recent ECCAS summit in Chad, the new regime in CAR was put under pressure to hold elections within 18 months. As interesting as these developments are, the cycle of violence in CAR has been blamed in part on the complicity of certain heads of regional states with undisclosed interests in the conflict and even their participation in the peace agreement negotiations. These latter cannot be said to have benefited significantly from inputs from the warring parties. Thus, the failure of the peace and ceasefire agreement is traceable to the failure of the regional leadership to accommodate the views of the warring factions, since political solutions should come from the people within the CAR. Also, the relapse into violence and setback to the peace process may have had tacit support from forces within ECCAS. It has been argued that the ECCAS peacekeeping force that quashed the first Seleka rebellion in December 2012 turned its back on the second rebellion (Dersso 2013). Of course, other challenges confront ECCAS, such as poor internal governance and weak finances, so that the organisation is excessively dependent on external assistance and support. Responsibility for the African peacekeeping force in the CAR (MISCA) was transferred to the AU primarily because the ECCAS force lacked the capacity and credibility to mediate effectively. However, the AU's hands-off approach in the negotiation and implementation of the Libreville agreement is also to blame (Dersso 2013), as is its initial overestimation of ECCAS capacity.

In West Africa, the Accord de Non-Aggression et d'Assistance en Matière de Défense (ANAD) was signed in June 1977 by Burkina Faso, Mali, Mauritania, Niger, Senegal, Côte d'Ivoire and Togo. Benin and Guinea were granted observer status. ANAD's main objective was to promote security and stability to enhance economic development. It was not a supranational body, and nor did it develop military policy. It was clearly a defensive alliance, and an attack on any member would be interpreted as an attack on the entire alliance (Alao 2000). Its mode of operation includes dialogue and negotiation to resolve conflicts among members, and, if necessary, the deployment of a peace intervention force. Also, the accord stipulated that an external attack on a member state would entail the following actions: a search for a diplomatic solution, to be followed by an imposition of sanctions short of force, and finally, the use of armed force to counter the aggression. However, today ANAD has transcended its initial mission and includes elements of high-level integration such as common policy formulation and cooperation on broader human security issues.

Notably, where sub-regional mechanisms have recorded appreciable successes in conflict management and resolution, as in the case of ECOWAS/ECOMOG in West Africa, this is arguably because due regard has been paid to issues of good governance and democratisation (Sesay 2002). Some of the principles espoused in the revised ECOWAS treaty and other major declarations on conflicts in West Africa underscore that democratisation coupled with responsive and responsible governance are the most effective conflict-management tools. By contrast, where sub-regional conflict management mechanisms do not give due consideration to governance and democracy, the returns on investment have been rather low. SADC in some respects is a case of lack of consensus among member states on how to deal with human rights, democratisation and good governance issues.

While some attention has been given to regional integration in Africa, and by extension to regional collective security systems, there is still no convincing evidence of serious commitment by sub-regional integration schemes to continental integration. From the pioneering activities of the ECA towards regional integration, through the LPA, the Abuja Treaty, to recent AU and NEPAD initiatives, sub-regional organisations are conceived as important building blocks in continental integration. However, beyond rhetorical declarations in support of pan-Africanism and African unity, sub-regional organisations have subtly resisted continental integration. The divisions between African leaders who favour a top-down or a bottom-up approach has negative consequence for the direction of regionalism in Africa. The issue is not so much the relevance of sub-regional schemes as building blocks but how to organise their activities and to reduce frictions between them and the continental body. Until recently, when Ms. Dlamini-Zuma took over as the AUC chairperson, the relationship between the AU and SADC was not smooth. By contrast, the AU is well received by IGAD, whose member states prefer it to Ethiopia's influence in the Horn. In West Africa, the AU is not as popular, especially after the Mali experience, which increased interest among ECOWAS member states in a more effective sub-regional organisation rather than a domineering AU. Also, in West Africa, where it is considered the undisputed regional hegemon, Nigeria is seemingly intolerant of a South African presence. Predictably, these suspicions and rivalries have serious implications for coordination and collaboration between the AU and the sub-regional organisations in operationalising collective security on the continent.

Since the end of the Cold War, much has been done to export neoliberal values beyond Western societies, and with notable success. In this context, significant pressures were placed on Africa's authoritarian governments to embark on political reforms culminating in different forms of liberal democratic transition (Bratton and Van de Walle 1997). For their part, Western countries were set on reproducing liberal democracy by giving overwhelming support to Western liberal social values, specifically respect for the rule of law, individual freedom and civil liberty and electoral competition. Consequently, bilateral and multilateral donors, as well as international development agencies such as the World Bank and UNDP, made facilities available to governments and NGOs to ensure democracy and good governance in developing countries. For countries needing aid, trade concessions and other development assistance, however, his meant having to satisfy Western political conditions and, in most cases, adopt liberal democratic principles. It was in this context that many African countries transitioned from authoritarian and dictatorship-type regimes to liberal democracy. Unfortunately, the transitions did not run their full course in most African countries. Instead, they were fast-tracked by discredited African power elites, which tactically defused the rising social consciousness among the masses and then facilitated the inauguration of foreign-aided reformist agendas that never guaranteed genuine democracy.

The initial euphoria about the global success of liberal democracy was short-lived. The world recorded significant growth in the number of elected governments, but many new democracies – most of them in Africa – have been labelled by the West as "incomplete democratic transitions" and "illiberal democracies," despite the introduction of constitutions, legislatures and electoral systems. The transition did not result in improved living conditions for the citizenry. Indeed, there have been many similar assessments and evaluation reports on democracy and governance in Africa by international donors, as well as a growing number of anthologies on the failure of democracy in Africa (Diamond 1996). The central question is why the democratisation wave of the 1990s recorded less impressive accomplishments in Africa than, for instance, in Eastern Europe and other parts of the world.

Nonetheless, regional and sub-regional organisations in Africa have put in place several instruments to promote constitutionalism and democratisation. This is important, especially for a continent whose armed conflicts are often traceable to constitutional matters such as forceful changes of government, military coups, election cancellations, etc. Interestingly, the AU's Constitutive Act prohibits any member state in which there is an unconstitutional transfer of power from participating in AU activities. The AU has thus been able to condemn military takeovers and initiate transitions to democracy in some African countries. When President Bingu wa Mutharika of Malawi died, the AU insisted that the constitutional provisions on succession be complied with and that Vice President Joyce Banda take over the presidency. Similarly, it condemned the coup in Mali and demanded that a civilian government be installed to pave the way for democratic elections. Another recent case was the suspension of Egypt following the military overthrow of the government of President Morsi in July 2013. Suspension is fast becoming the AU's usual response to interruptions of constitutional rule in member states and is generally lifted once a country has held a free election, as in Madagascar, Mali and Mauritania. It is interesting to note that the AU, ECOWAS and SADC have also been actively involved in ensuring free and fair elections in several countries, both by way of election monitoring and mediating electoral conflicts. Examples of such interventions include Kenya, Togo and Zimbabwe.

These demonstrable changes in the commitment of African states to constitutionalism are also apparent in ECOWAS, which has applied its Protocol on Good Governance against unconstitutional regimes in West Africa, but with varying degrees of success. Predictably, the AU's application of constitutionalism has not been without challenges. With regard to the Arab Spring, there were debates in the PSC on how to apply the principle of suspension in the case of the overthrow of dictators in Tunisia and Egypt. In the end, it was decided that the constitutionalism principle should be interpreted in favour of democracy rather than of buttressing the status quo. The AU, which viewed the Libyan crisis as a civil war demanding mediation, has been severely criticised for not responding more promptly.

According to UNECA's *African Governance Report III*, the continent has made only marginal progress in governance. The report shows declining governance scores relative to the previous year, with no improvement in democratisation in particular. This is evident in Mali, which recently experienced a military coup and armed conflict, while the democratic transitions in North Africa, notably in Tunisia, Algeria, Egypt, Libya and Morocco, have not progressed much either. Moreover, while elections have been held in many countries, their regularity has not prevented election-related violence, as witness Côte d'Ivoire, DRC, Kenya, Nigeria and Zimbabwe.

The AU has several special programmes to help quicken its operations. These include NEPAD, APRM and the CSSDCA. NEPAD has now been officially incorporated into the AU as a "technical body" and its APRM is the main AU programme for promoting good governance and accountability in Africa. The APRM was approved by the NEPAD implementation committee and endorsed by the AU Summit in Durban in July 2002. In principle, the APRM represents the channel through which African countries can take corrective steps towards the sustainable development of the continent.

Although the APRM looks at four thematic areas (democracy and good political governance, economic governance and management, corporate governance, and socioeconomic development), it is generally tilted towards economic issues. Participation in the APRM is open to all AU member states, and there seems to be an overwhelming consensus among them that the APRM is a welcome development. In 2012, there were 31 APRM countries, with 15 countries already peer-reviewed (Mehler et al. 2013: 7). Although the APRM is still at an early stage of implementation, there are already signs of impact in terms of governance gains from countries that have inaugurated the process and embarked on reforms. For instance, the second progress report for Uganda shows progress in private sector promotion and infrastructure development. Similarly, Burkina Faso's third report on the national programme of action highlights the government's commitment to developing the export sector as well as its mediation and conflict-resolution efforts in West Africa (Mehler et al. 2013: 8).

However, the APRM is bedevilled by inadequate funding, non-involvement of civil society and lack of political will. The latter is indeed a major obstacle, since the peer review process is voluntary, lacking sanctions and effective enforcement mechanisms. Also, the APRM is not sufficiently concerned with early warning signs (Mehler et al. 2013: 7). This is a major limitation, given the frequency and extent of armed conflicts in Africa. Because of this, some have asked whether the ARRM was actually designed with Africa in mind. There is also concern that NEPAD and its components reflect the preferences of the Washington Consensus rather than the Africans who are its supposed beneficiaries (Adesina et al. 2006).

While African leaders fast-tracked the birth of the AU, there is no evidence of the involvement in the process of different categories of African peoples. Only a "few African leaders chose to open the subject of a new union for public discussion within their countries" (Packer and Rukare 2002: 365). A survey conducted in 15 African countries in 2002-03 shows that only 49 per cent of respondents had heard of continental bodies such as the AU (even though the questionnaire used its former name, OAU) or even their regional economic community, namely SADC, EAC and ECOWAS.[2] The consequence of this for the execution of regional programmes and collective security initiatives is that they may lack domestic support in many African countries. A case in point is Nigeria's ongoing generous support for ECOWAS peacekeeping operations in West Africa. At home, successive Nigerian governments have been criticised in the media for unjustified investment in such operations.

Some in the Nigerian foreign policy community feel that Nigeria has not been duly acknowledged for its role in restoring peace and stability in war-torn

---

2. See "Africans' Views of International Organizations," Afrobarometer Briefing Paper No. 8, August 2003.

Liberia, Togo, Sierra Leone and São Tomé and Príncipe. They argue that despite Nigeria's laudable investment in external relations, especially with African countries, its external image continues to suffer greatly. The recent Nigeria-led ECOWAS intervention in Mali was not favourably received by many Nigerians, who felt that President Goodluck Jonathan had no business sending troops abroad to fight while Nigeria was facing national security threats from Boko Haram, youth militants in the Niger Delta and sectarian violence on Jos Plateau. The drastic reduction in Nigeria's forces in Mali may be connected with domestic pressures on the government for that intervention. Similarly, in South Africa President Zuma had to recall South African troops from CAR following the death of 13 of them during peace support-operations in that country. The deaths provoked critical comments from citizens, who questioned the rationale for sending South African troops to far-away CAR, despite logistical challenges.

African armed forces have been engaged in peace support operations, especially under UN mandates. However, many questions remain about their technical capacity to intervene militarily to ensure and maintain peace in conflict zones on the continent. With the possible exception of South Africa, Nigeria and Egypt, many African armies lack combat-readiness, armaments and mobilisation and deployment speed, and are hardly up to complex peace operations. For instance, ECOMOG peace operations in Liberia and Sierra Leone confronted a number of military challenges. There were also allegations of unruly behaviour by soldiers: ECOMOG troops were reportedly implicated in terrible crimes in Liberia in the 1990s. South Africa is credited with having strong military forces, but was recently humiliated in the CAR. Aside from inadequate technical capabilities, poor funding for multilateral peace operations by the AU and sub-regional organisations is a major hindrance in the execution of their conflict resolution and management strategies.

The complicity of state and non-state actors in regional conflicts is a serious challenge, especially where such actors incline towards parochial nationalism or are interested parties in the conflict. In some instances, the problem is how to contain unhealthy rivalry among states within the region, or how to manage changes in the regional balance of power in the aftermath of intervention. There is also the challenge of how to check the expansionist aspirations of some regional powers that may want to exploit conflict to their own advantage. Some illustrations are useful here. Nigeria was rumoured to be interested in protecting President Samuel Doe of Liberia. Rwanda and Uganda were accused of having links with rebels in the DRC.

Lack of consensus among states in the sub-region can also create difficulties. For example, Nigeria faced initial opposition from Côte d'Ivoire and other ECOWAS member states over the legality of ECOMOG's intervention in Liberia. Similarly, recently ECOWAS countries were divided over whether the sub-regional body should intervene in conflicts in Côte d'Ivoire. While Nigeria supported intervention, Ghana was openly unwilling to deploy troops. This inability to act in a unified manner was a major impediment to resolving the conflict in Côte d'Ivoire. In East Africa, Ethiopia's and Kenya's interventions in Somalia in 2006 and 2011 respectively were deeply problematic and had less to do with stabilisation than with promoting their national interests. The AU proposed that neighbouring countries with interests in Somalia should not be part of AMISOM. This wisdom was, however, abandoned when the AU and UN agreed to include the Kenyan troops already in Somalia in the mission.

IGAD's ongoing mediation in the conflict between the government of South Sudan and the armed opposition is not making the desired progress partly because of the complicity of some countries in the sub-region. For example, the Ugandan army allegedly supported South Sudan government troops in January 2014 in retaking major towns recently seized by the opposition. The Ugandan government claimed that the military mission was to evacuate over 200,000 stranded Ugandan nationals. Beyond the legal and diplomatic niceties, the suspicion of Uganda's military support for the South Sudan government may have impeded mediation by IGAD. Although an IGAD-brokered cessation of hostilities agreement was signed, which stipulates that "armed groups and allied forces invited by either side" should be redeployed and/or progressively withdrawn, IGAD has not been able to withdraw its troops from South Sudan.

Similarly, the concern that Chad was using MISCA, the new AU-led mission to the CAR, to further its own regional ambitions cannot be easily dismissed given rumours of Chad's complicity in the overthrow of President François Bozizé. Also, the perception by some parties to the conflict in Mali that the Algerian government is a biased mediator has not helped the peace process in the country. In January 2014, a meeting between armed groups and the Malian government was organised by the Algeria. However, the Mouvement Arabe de l'Azawad (MAA), Mouvement National pour la Liberation de l'Azawad and Mouvement Arabe de l'Azawad declined to attend, accusing Algiers of inviting pro-government MAA representatives.

Aside from the role of national leaders and governments in conflicts within sub-regions, the influence and interests of actors outside the regions have serious consequences for conflict resolution and peacebuilding, especially where those actors do not enjoy the confidence of all the parties to the conflict. A case in point is the growing interest of ECOWAS and some Western countries, notably the UK, France and US in the fight against the insurgency in northern Nigeria. The Nigerian government is seeking assistance from notably the US and France to quash the Boko Haram insurgency. Through the US-sponsored Pan-Sahel Initiative and the Trans-Saharan Counterterrorism Partnership, the US has been building the capacity of certain West African countries, including Nigeria, to combat terrorism. France, on its own, is scaling up its military presence in the Sahel. However, the perception among the insurgents of France as an enemy nation may encourage them to extend their activities to Benin, Cameroon, Niger and other francophone countries abutting Nigeria, bringing further instability to West and Central Africa.

Also, many foreign-supported counter-insurgency operations have not resulted in much peace and stability. The defeat of the US-backed Malian forces by insurgents after the military overthrew the elected government is one such case. Similarly, in CAR US-supported forces were unable to prevent a rebel group from ousting the president. Also, the Western-backed transitional government in Libya has not been able to check the militias.

New global dynamics have made a regionalist approach to conflict management more desirable. The world is today witnessing various forms of religious fundamentalism and ethnic nationalism resulting in more intra-state conflicts than the UN collective security system had envisaged. UN peacekeeping, apart from being overstretched, gives more recognition to sovereign states than non-state actors, a preference that is seemingly anachronistic and unsuitable for today. These and other factors have limited UN peacekeeping interventions. In the last decade, there has been no significant increase in multilateral peace operations under UN auspices. Also, there seems to be a reduction in personnel serving in multilateral operations. Governments have become more critical of spending on peace operations and demand more accountability. The UNSC has responded with stricter conditions and requirements to ensure effectiveness and efficiency. Predictably, UN peace operations have narrowed considerably, concentrating on achievable tasks within a set timeframe. Also, there is increased attention to value for money in recent UN multilateral peace operations. Inter-mission cooperation to achieve common goals across countries is being encouraged, as with the UN Mission in Liberia (UNMIL) and UN Operation in Côte d'Ivoire (UNOCI). Dwindling UN resources no doubt affects UN capacity for comprehensive peace operations. One observable trend is the neglect to protect civilians in UN peace operations, as demonstrated in UN operations in Côte d'Ivoire (SIPRI 62).

Global actors have been linked with peace and security issues in Africa in several ways, including providing assistance that reflects their economic and political interests. Africa is of geostrategic importance to major international actors, including as a source of natural resources such as oil and strategic minerals. In recent times, anti-terrorism has been added to the motives for intervening in African conflicts. These interests also dictate the direction of the support provided by members of the international community for the management and resolution of African conflicts. While during the Cold War it was possible to predict the behaviour of powerful nations in terms of their interests and support, the post Cold War period appears to be witnessing inconsistencies in the reactions and responses of these same actors. For example, how does one reconcile the prompt reactions to the uprising in Libya with the silence in Washington and Brussels over the revolt against Ben Ali of Tunisia?

Arguably, the US has remained committed to its strategic interests in Middle East and North Africa. Thus its responses have been based largely on its assessment of individual events vis-à-vis its national interests. However, in Libya it would appear Washington was committed to regime change, given the support it gave Transitional National Council.[3] Also, the US initially supported the Brotherhood's Freedom and Justice Party in Egypt possibly in order to advance its "War on Terror," which the Brotherhood was believed to be willing to help prosecute. The US recently announced that it has budgeted $ 101 million to help African forces and France re-establish security in the CAR. The announcement came after its initial promise to set aside $ 40 million for MISCA in November 2013. Other US assistance consists of military aid for foreign troops stationed in the CAR, plus $ 15 million in humanitarian aid. The scaling up of US investment in regional peace initiatives in CAR requires further interrogation in order to distinguish between altruism and self-interested power-seeking by a hegemonic power.

Similarly, France's responses to conflicts in Côte d'Ivoire, Mali, DRC and most recently the CAR must be understood in the context of its strategic political and economic interests in Africa, including existing and future investments in mineral resources in DRC, Cameroon and Chad. In this regard, France's military presence in Africa is being consolidated through the reorganisation of its 3,000 troops in the Sahel. In a similar gesture, Germany announced that troops would be sent to Mali as part of a Franco-German brigade under the aegis of the EU and would also support an EU peacekeeping mission in the CAR. Germany is not alone. Belgium, Italy, the Netherlands, Portugal, Spain and the UK are all involved in the EU- training programme for the Malian military.

The activities of China, Russia and other emerging powers in Africa have implications for peace and security on the continent. While most emerging powers are allegedly less bothered about the internal affairs of African countries and espouse principles of non-interference and respect for sovereignty, they are not completely divorced from peace and security issues on the continent. The division between the P3 (Britain, France and the US) and P2 (Russia and China) over the role of the UNSC in the Libyan crisis was reminiscent of East-West rivalry in the Cold War era. There is as yet no reason to suggest bloc voting by the new global powers in the UNSC. However, further research into the geostrategic interests of the P5 and the BRICS will help us understand the appearance of difference between the two power blocs as well as how to promote and ensure global governance especially within the framework of the UNSC, with its mandate to maintain international peace and security.

Apart from China's activities in the UNSC multilateral platform, its contribution to peacekeeping and peacebuilding operations in Africa is seen as merely opportunistic and is provoking concern in some circles. China's contributions to UN peacekeeping operations in Liberia, Sudan and Darfur, like

3. Libya's Transitional National Council has a sizeable number of members from the Muslim Brotherhood and Islamists such as the Libyan Islamic Fighting Group. The Brotherhood was set to play a significant role in the new government in Libya and received substantial support from US allies in the Arab world.

its support for peace operations globally, are connected to its status and interests as a rising global power. However, the contradictions in China's approach to peace support in Africa are best demonstrated with this example: China provided a large contingent of peacekeeping troops to Liberia. However, China was also perpetuating and sustaining the despotic rule of Charles Taylor through its illicit buying of timber. Some argue that China's economic activities in Africa contribute to conditions favourable to violent conflict on the continent. This was most clearly demonstrated in China's role in the conflict between Sudan and South Sudan. Rather than pressure Khartoum to adopt more forward-looking positions, Beijing, on the pretext of non-interference, mostly engaged in palliative measures that never challenged the Sudanese state. However, after 2006 China influenced Sudan into accepting the deployment of peacekeepers in Darfur. Similarly, in 2008 it pressured the governments of DRC and Rwanda to resolve the conflict in eastern DRC. Apart from investing in Sudanese oil, China is Sudan's main source of military equipment and arms, including helicopters, tanks, fighter planes, bombers, rocket-launched grenades and machines guns. Also on Darfur, both China and Russia blocked many UN resolutions meant to put pressure on the Sudanese government. Russia is Sudan's strongest investment partner and also its strategic political ally. Such realities colour both China's and Russia's support for peace and security in Africa. Nonetheless, China and Russia have provided support to the AU in the promotion of peace and security on the continent. China has provided the AU with US$ 1.8 million for its peacekeeping mission in Sudan and given financial support to the AU mission in Somali and West Africa's sub-regional peace fund (Saferworld 2011: v).

EU assistance for Africa peace and security operations is by far the most predictable and comprehensive. Examples include support for the AU peacekeeping mission in Darfur, the CEMAC mission in the CAR, and for the AU's institutional capacity building programme. In addition, the EU directly supports direct international intervention within the framework the EU-Africa strategy. Also, the EU allocated € 50 million from the African Peace Facility (APF) to support the deployment of AFISMA to Mali and other peace operations by the AU and African regional organisations, such as AMISOM in Somalia and MICOPAX in CAR. Other forms of EU security engagement include the police mission (EUPOL) and the security sector reform programme. For example, the European Commission supports the training in 17 centres of police, civilian and military personnel that can be deployed in African peace support operations as part of the African Standby Force. In December 2013, the EU announced it would provide € 12.5 million to improve the management of African-led peace support operations, especially in satellite communications and IT facilities, which in turn will improve communications between the AU, the sub-regional organisations and peace missions deployed at country level.

Most EU funding of APSA has been from the APF and has focused on the military activities of AU and REC peace-support operations. Since 2004, the EU has provided € 1.1 billion in support through the APF. This has contributed to the success of several African-led peace operations, notably AMISOM and AFISMA. Also, the APF supported a number of mediation and conflict-prevention actions. It contributed to the AU's high-level implementation panel for Sudan and South Sudan and the development of more comprehensive political dialogue between the EU and Africa in the area of peace and security. However, the EU's funding approach is not without challenges. First, selective EU funding makes it difficult for other areas of need within APSA to be addressed. Also, there are delays and late responses due in part to over-bureaucratisation of processes and procedures. As with foreign assistance generally, recipient choice and preference come second to donor priorities and considerations, and EU support is no exception. It is a truism in international relations that foreign assistance serves a complex set of objectives that may not be mutually consistent.

There is also a new global consensus on democratisation, good governance and human rights, and the global North has emerged as its undisputed champion since the end of the Cold War. One consequence for countries of the global South, especially those dependent on external assistance and trade concessions, is aid fatigue in the face of tough conditionalities. For example, aid seekers must now adhere to liberal democratic principles and possibly keep scorecards on transparent and accountable governance. The EU has since the late 1980s been prominently associated with the promotion of human rights and liberal democratic values, and this has affected its relationships with partners in the South. For example, the political dimension of development cooperation has gained much prominence in partnership relationships. This can be seen in the EU-ACP Conventions, the Cotonou Partnership Agreement and lately the EU-Africa Strategic Partnership, under which the EU provides peace support operations in addition to assistance initiatives. There are concerns that continuing EU support for such operations will depend on the smooth running of the broad cooperation frameworks as well as the political conditionalities associated with the operations.

Admittedly, the relationship between African regional organisations and the UN as regards conflict management and resolution has improved somewhat since the end of the Cold War. There is, however, room for improvement. While the UN can be credited with the conceptual and operational development of the principle of R2P (responsibility to protect), regional organisations come across as the main channel for actualising the new logic. Ordinarily, this should make effective partnership between the UN and regional organisations mutually desirable and therefore an easy walk! In practice, however, this paradigm shift in managing and resolving conflicts is not yet fully expressed in the relationship between the UN, AU and RECs. The case of Côte d'Ivoire was indeed revealing in this respect. African states were generally uncomfortable with the way in which UN and French forces carried out the military operations that resulted in the arrest of President Laurent Gbagbo. Both the AU chairman and Thabo Mbeki, former AU mediator in Côte d'Ivoire, declared the military intervention unjustified. For Mbeki, what happened was simply "the UN entrenching former colonial powers on our continent" (Mbeki 2011). UN Secretary General Ban Ki-moon defended UN intervention, claiming that the forces acted strictly in accordance with R2P based on UNSC Resolution 1975 of 30 March 2011 (Schori 2015). Effective global-regional partnership is possible through increased consultation, cooperation and collaboration between the UN and African regional organisations, but the dominant actors and players must change and become more supportive of the regionalist approach to international security and peace.

The case of Libya arguably demonstrated how lack of consultation between UN and AU could hamper the development and consolidation of global-regional partnerships for peace in Africa. The UN and AU not only adopted different approaches based on their perceptions of the issues in the conflict, they also made no effort to coordinate their conflict-resolution strategies. Consequently, the AU felt deliberately sidelined, a circumstance interpreted in many African circles as conspiracy to ignore African efforts to resolve the conflict in Libya. There were also other cases of division in the international community. The response to the military coup in Guinea-Bissau, for instance, had the AU, EU and UN pitched against ECOWAS, which mediated the setting up of a transitional government, which was denied recognition by the UN, AU and EU.

The AU wants to be recognised as the main regional organ for collective security in Africa. This may bring the AU into confrontation with the UNSC, which does not yet appear willing to cede its mandate for maintaining global peace and security to regional organisations, even though its acknowledges that the latter have significant influence on conflicts within their regions, and credits them with a good understanding of regional dynamics. The UN has its own challenges. With approximately 120, 000 military, police and civilian peacekeepers and a budget of almost US$ 8 billion per year, it is understandable why it is less disposed towards taking on more of the burden from regional organisations (Bam 2012: 8). Thus while the UNSC is seemingly unwilling to share its powers with regional organisations, it is seriously constrained by inadequate resources to operationalize its mandate. Besides, the UN post-conflict peacekeeping approach requires a ceasefire agreement and the prior consent of the parties to the conflict. This does not lend itself readily to the realities of African conflicts, such as in Rwanda, Darfur and Somalia. Also, it appears that the UN is less appreciative of the complexity of African conflicts, including the regional dimensions. For instance, the UNSC mandate for military action in Libya eventually forced Islamist insurgents out of the country, only for them to regroup strongly in northern Mali with the prospect of spreading to other parts of the Sahel. Similarly, UNSC delayed sanctioning military action, waiting almost endlessly for ECOWAS to come up with a plan to drive the Islamist militias out of northern Mali. At the end of the day, the serious humanitarian crisis that was feared would come with military intervention was not averted.

There are other areas of growing tension in the relationship between African countries and the UN that may affect continuing cooperation. One can argue that the UNSC is much less responsive to changes than other UN institutions. First, the resistance by the permanent UNSC members to developing country demands that the UN be restructured to allow for greater democratisation exemplifies the desire to preserve the status quo in the UN, and by extension the architecture of global security. Second, there is the lingering allegation of bias by the International Criminal Court in its handling of cases involving African leaders, and also the complaint about the UNSC's lack of representativeness.

Conclusions, policy recommendations and research priorities

Contrary to the expectations regarding the end of the Cold War, the anticipated peace dividend has so far eluded us. The world is still drenched in violent conflicts, most of them intra-state and actual or potential springboards for regional conflicts. Added to these are new forms of violence such as piracy, human trafficking and terrorism, with many such incidents occurring in Africa and having severe regional dimensions. These and other related developments have far-reaching implications for the principles and practice of peacebuilding. More than ever, peace and development are intimately linked. They are regarded by the UN and other international actors as inseparable goals. This has significantly influenced the emergence of new conceptions of peace, security and development.

Nonetheless, there are still issues that require further attention in the link between peace and development. One is the relationship between conflict and global development. Recently, Tillman Bruck has drawn our attention to the unwarranted "silence on security, conflict and peace in global development," observing that "none of the Millennium Development Goals refers to peace or security" (2013: 1). Similarly, previous African programmes for economic development such as the LPA, NAI, MAP, Omega Plan and the new NEPAD have no frameworks and indicators relating peace and security to development goals. While NEPAD has clauses that focus on common, comprehensive security issues, and some elements of conflict prevention and mitigation, such as capacity building for conflict management and an early warning system (NEPAD 2001), these measures do not address security as a primary concern. It should be possible to broaden the AU/NEPAD Peer Review Mechanism to include indicators that define and measure armed conflicts and appropriately project them as threats and risks to development processes and outcomes. In this way, targets and benchmarks for peace and security can be developed to guide states and regional actors. Also, this approach calls for mainstreaming analysis of conflict prevention at all levels of development planning and implementation.

So far, I have presented peacebuilding as an integrated process whose elements include prevention and resolution of violent conflicts, consolidation of peace once violence has been reduced through systematic mediation and reconciliation, and post-conflict reconstruction with a view to avoiding relapses into violent conflict. There are different levels in a conflict, and conflict resolution must consider all of them and align them with the attainment of sustainable peace. Thus, interventions by the UN, regional and sub-regional organisations, donors and development partners should emphasise commitment to "positive peace," which, in addition to the absence of violence, seeks post-conflict socioeconomic security, equity and participation. For instance, interventions and peace operations should target the provision of basic services in conflict zones while they encourage the civil population to own the peace process. It is thus my submission that conflicts in all their ramifications must be understood as development issues, and their resolution as development practice. It is in this context that the political and social dimensions of peace processes are seen as complementary in making peace a lasting outcome. As development practice, peacebuilding, in addition to institutional reform in politics, law and economics, should pay due attention to sociological factors such as gender, civil society, religion, the deconstruction of violent masculinities, restorative justice, emotions, hope, forgiveness, truth recovery, social memory and public victimhood (Brewer 2010). It is my opinion that the broad social and political issues that are at the base of many conflicts in Africa can be identified and highlighted in this conceptual model as issues in African development discourse.

The enlargement of internal conflicts beyond the original warring parties is now a common feature of armed conflicts. Another observable trend in the post-Cold War international system is the increasing popularity of regional approaches to preventing and managing conflicts among states and non-state actors. In Africa, there is growing awareness that the pursuit of economic development by regional integration schemes is only possible in a peaceful atmosphere. While the quest for *the* theoretical model for measuring the impact of regional cooperation on conflict management mechanisms continues, there is overwhelming evidence of the impact of regions and regional cooperation on conflict management mechanisms (Swanstrom 2002). This is true of both Western and non-Western regions, where there are many illustrations of strong interaction between regional cooperation and conflict management. In the case of Africa, it seems that countries have given expanded interpretation to Chapter VIII of the 1945 UN Charter, which spells out the critical role of regional organisations in global collective security to accommodate "African solutions to African problems." In the foregoing discussion, I have highlighted the peace and development nexus, and its centrality in regional approaches to peace in Africa. African leaders have themselves come to see peace and development as going hand in hand. This logic underscores the roles played by the AU and also the RECs in promoting peace and security on the continent. Similarly, the founders of NEPAD identified peace as one of two prerequisites for African development. It is important, however, that individual states embrace national development programmes that enhance national and regional peace and security. At the heart of this project is good governance.

The importance of the global context cannot be overemphasised. Thus in this lecture, I have drawn attention to the international environment in terms of the opportunities and challenges for the development and consolidation of regional collective security in Africa. Several international "friends of the continent" are responding positively by supporting African regional and sub-regional organisations in promoting the regionalist approach to conflict resolution. The adoption of the G8 Africa Action Plan at Kananaskis in 2002 was remarkable in this regard. It sets out comprehensive G8 commitments focused on peace support operations in Africa. Also, under the EU Strategy for Africa, EU members have consistently funded the implementation of the European Security and Defence Action Plan to support peace and security in Africa. Some of the new global powers have also supported AU mechanisms for peace and stability, but they have shown less interest in sub-regional organisations.

African regional integration schemes have performed unimpressively for reasons associated with the absence of peace and security. Interestingly, today there is growing support for pursuing peace and development in Africa through regional approaches to the extent that the success or failure of regional integration is assessed on the basis of its contribution to regional peace and security. This is important, especially in view of earlier concerns like those expressed by Fantu Cheru that the continent "lacked the necessary commitment and organized effort required to resolve conflicts … The glaring lack of continental and subregional institutional mechanisms and the absence of a common security infrastructure make prevention and resolution of conflicts difficult" (2002: 198). While at the continental level there have been efforts to ensure that adequate institutional frameworks exist for some of the new initiatives, at the sub-regional levels there is a near-absence of institutional frameworks and structures. Also, the AU and sub-regional organisations face financial and logistical challenges. In the absence of institutional structures, conflict resolution initiatives have mostly been ad hoc. The SADC best illustrates this limitation. It lacks integrated systems, processes and methods to deal with issues such as human rights and the advancement of democracy and good governance. The lack of consensus among member states on "how the Organ should relate to the SADC Summit," coupled with the lack of "political will and institutional capacity" has not helped SADC to evolve into a regional security community (Dieter et al. 2001: 65). Also, ideological divisions among member states have continued to hamper the work of the Organ (Dieter et al. 2001: 65). For example, while Angola, Zimbabwe and Namibia favour military solutions to conflict, South Africa, Mozambique and to some extent Zambia support the principles and objectives of the SADC Organ. Also, the absence of effective early warning systems and risk assessment capacities in many sub-regional and regional security arrangements in Africa seriously weakens their conflict-prevention potential.

The organisational and decision-making capabilities necessary for managing peace support processes and operations are still not adequately available within the AU and RECs. For instance, African conflicts require conflict resolution strategies and operations with sufficient authority for the AU to intervene in international, transnational and intrastate conflicts. Similarly, the authority and power to enforce sanctions and ensure compliance with resolutions is highly necessary. Also, prevention of violent conflict requires the technical capacity for pre-emptive intervention in the early stages of conflicts. The AU, however, requires authority to carry out such intervention without the invitation or approval of host governments. Other issues inhibiting timely and coherent AU responses to violent conflicts, as witnessed in the Libyan case, need to be addressed. The AU PSC on 10 March 2010 rejected "any foreign military intervention" in Libya. However, barely a week later, the three non-permanent African members of the UNSC voted in favour Resolution 1973.

The desirability of involving African organisations in the management and resolution of conflicts on the continent is not contested. However, only limited success has been recorded in this regard. Despite obvious shortcomings, regional organisations are still largely the primary units of security and conflict management for Africa. The UN and other international actors have explicitly approved increased engagement by regional and sub-regional organisations in conflict management. Also, African states themselves now recognise that they have to rely less on Northern generosity to manage African conflicts.

Effective continental and regional cooperation will continue to be useful for peace support operations in Africa. On one hand, the prospect of Pan-African and regional cooperation seems bright. A strong sense of solidarity is evident in some new continent-wide initiatives. Indeed, many countries in Africa are increasingly committed to Pan-African regional integration. Given the untiring efforts of these countries as well as renewed interest by political elites in Pan-Africanism and the African Renaissance, one can conclude that these efforts will continue into the future. However, such efforts need to be supported by a new orientation and thinking that transcend the previous dominant notion of national sovereignty, which rendered the OAU impotent and incapable of promoting genuine Pan-African cooperation and integration. The new thinking must therefore promote good governance measured in term of effective and efficient delivery of public goods and services to the majority of citizens. Beyond the efforts of individual African governments in this regard, there should be a regional strategy to promote good governance. The AU and to some extent NEPAD share this new thinking. Good governance can significantly reduce violent conflicts. Also the development of transnational, regional civil society through networks of groups across national borders should be encouraged. Such platforms can promote Pan-African cooperation that will support collective regional security through peace education and other forms of civic engagement. Also, African regional organisations' engagement with global institutions on consolidating the regionalist approach to peace and security in Africa should be encouraged. Efforts made by the UN and its agencies are commendable and should also be encouraged.

Similarly, the international community should broaden its notion of preventive diplomacy in Africa to include support in addressing new forms of violence, and specifically the development of comprehensive national and regional early warning systems. For example, illicit trafficking and transnational organised crime, notably in East and West Africa, constitute serious threats. Also, concerted efforts are required to check illicit trade networks and terrorist organisations. In 2011, Africa experienced 978 terrorist attacks, an 11 per cent increase over 2010 and mainly attributable to the increase in Boko Haram attacks (from 31 in 2010 to 136 in 2011) in Nigeria (US Department of State 2012). There are several initiatives by African regional organisations to address cross-border crime. The 360th AU Peace and Security meeting on 22 March 2013 addressed issues of preventive diplomacy, and noted the significant reduction in conflicts in Africa as a result of collective AU efforts supported by international partners. While this is commendable, powerful nations, notably the US States, Russia and key EU members need to support regional and sub-regional initiatives on the ground by providing technical and financial resources.

The importance of effective global-regional partnerships in the management of international security cannot be overstressed. To effectively address the peace and security challenge in Africa, there is a need to engage a network of global and regional actors as opposed to a single institution. This was exemplified in Liberia (UNMIL), and the joint AU-UN and A2U Mission in Somalia with the support of UN, EU and other donors. With rising global consciousness of the R2P principle, the need to build effective global-regional partnerships for peace has become a major concern in the international system. However, there is much to be done to achieve a model of global-regional partnership in conflict resolution. There is no easy answer to the question of how far the UNSC should go to accommodate the demand of African states for African solutions to African problems. At present, the UNSC is in a particularly powerful position vis-à-vis Africa's regional and sub-regional organisations, but there are limits on how far the UNSC can go in ignoring the solutions preferred by African states without souring relations with them. Among the lessons learned from recent conflicts in Africa is the need for UNSC to be more realistic in its engagements with regional organisations. For instance, prompt mandates for ECOWAS and AU to undertake military action in northern Mali would have prevented the escalation of the conflict, especially when governments of advanced countries were shying away from troop deployment.

The AU's Constitutive Act supports engagement with African non-state institutions in resolving African conflicts. This suggests that civil society has an important role in shaping peace and security policies and processes. Without sufficient participation of civil society groups either in the political process or through adequate consultation, regional cooperation and integration efforts and initiatives risk becoming easy prey to sabotage. There are increasing opportunities in Africa for civil society organisations to engage in peace and security issues, although such organisations generally lack the technical capacity and experience to do so effectively. First, they lack the resource base and organisational capacity to engage government and other stakeholders. Second, many African governments have become increasingly intolerant of civil society organisations, especially in matters of peace and security, and the organisations do not have access to information about security. It is noteworthy that there are new initiatives within NEPAD and the AU to develop the capacities of African civil society organisations. These new initiatives, however, need to be translated into a concrete agenda and programme for civil society engagement with regional collective security structures and processes in Africa.

The culture and values of African peoples promote peace. Traditional institutions, grounded in indigenous social values and contexts, play significant roles in conflict resolution. For example, peace in the African cultural context reflects deep appreciation of the dialectical unity of social, economic and political processes. While some may argue that Africa has seen the largest number of international military interventions, the continent has great lessons to share on holistic approaches to peace and conflict management based on a deep sense of community that add value to mediation and arbitration processes, including political negotiations. Recently, a perceptive writer acknowledged this African value in this way:

> African experience is that wars are ended through political negotiation. Military intervention, with … the stated or unstated object of regime change or … total defeat of an insurgency, does not end conflicts, but at best mutates them and at worst escalates them. The African Union is not averse to using force – it typically is the first responder in the most difficult situations … But African practice underscores the importance of using force in support of a political-diplomatic strategy, not as an alternative … African experience has contributed … a number of guiding principles for conflict resolution, notably … insistence on all stakeholders being involved in negotiating a settlement. Were the Syrian conflict taking place on the African continent, all the neighbours would be engaged in a forum seeking a settlement. (de Waal 2013)

There are a number of successful applications of the African mode of conflict resolution that considers the conflict environment in its totality, and seeks more political than military solutions. The AMIB peacekeeping approach shows some social engagement with local communities in peacekeeping. One is tempted to agree with Abou Jeng (2012) that the relative peace in Somaliland is due to the ability of Somali traditional institutions to maintain peace. This lecture affirms the relevance of the traditional institutions as well as mediation and reconciliation practices of African societies.

Efforts by continental and sub-regional organisations to promote democratic governance in Africa are commendable. The AU, ECOWAS and SADC now acknowledge the essence of regular, open and fair elections, and have gone ahead to provide reasonable support to the electoral process in member states. For example, in December 2010 in Dakar, ECOWAS heads of state adopted the Supplementary Protocol on Democracy and Good Governance that stipulates that "every accession to power must be made through free, fair and transparent elections." There are also concerns about how to fight corruption and promote good governance at the regional level. The UNECA report *Striving for Good Governance for Africa* calls for measures to prevent African political parties from being "hijacked by the rich and influential." The AU Convention on Combating and Preventing Corruption (2003) acknowledges the importance of regulating private funding and calls on states to do so. Also, NEPAD has a peer review mechanism meant to hold African states accountable for their obligations, including obligations for good governance. The APRM's second objective includes "periodic political competition and opportunity for choice." Almost two decades have passed since the "third wave" of democratisation began to roll across sub-Saharan Africa and regular elections have become relatively well-established in many countries. The experience of many of Africa's new democracies, however, shows that it is possible to have elections without democracy. Existing initiatives need to be complemented by concrete good governance strategies that guarantee provision of public goods to the majority of citizens and thus reduce discontent among them.

Finally, further research is required to help African regional and sub-regional organisations and other stakeholders more precisely identify and define important issues in the link between development and collective security. For example, the roles and responsibilities of national, regional and other actors in peacebuilding need to be studied in more detail so as to understand the interests underlying the actors' behaviour. Such knowledge is useful in understanding, for instance, the complicity of certain actors in some of the violent conflicts in Africa. Similarly, in-depth study of the political economy of peace support operations in Africa should be encouraged and supported by critical stakeholders within and outside Africa. For example, what is the relationship between the domestic politics and the external behaviour of the core states leading peace missions in Africa? This should help to explain why some peace operations do not enjoy strong domestic support in participating countries. Research initiatives should necessarily consider the importance of domestic forces such as civil society to support or hinder peace processes. For example, while the impact of civil wars in Africa has become a popular research subject, the roles of the business community, organised private sectors and other components of civil society are often un-documented. Some aspects of peace and security largely depend on sufficient participation by civil society: the people and their associations, professional societies, farmers' groups, women's groups as well as political parties need to be carried along in the decision-making process. The modalities and procedures that best suit the African context need to be studied in greater detail.

Moreover, there is a need to generate more information to determine the logics and interests of external actors and their suitability for interventions in African conflicts. Other issues for in-depth research include the influence of the external environment on African conflicts. Also, efforts to promote the involvement of Africans in finding solutions to their problems should go beyond mere sloganeering to include scientific research, which entails data and information gathering, analysis and re-analysis. For example, while peace support operations are becoming common research subjects, studies on the politics and economics of peace support operations need to be encouraged.

The above prescriptions come with political ramifications that demand complex institutions and structures and extensive political will, as well as unity of objectives and commitments. First, political will is required among African leaders to collectively deal with peace- and security-threatening situations and conditions on the continent. Second, African leaders should support the existing structures and institutions of the regional and sub-regional organisations for the prevention, management and resolution of conflicts. Third, political will must be harnessed to produce an impressive record of African states' commitment to financial support for peace operations, timely contribution of troops and compliance with resolutions and decisions of regional and sub-regional organisations, among other things. It is through such serious commitment and dedication to African development that the continent's new image as a place of rising hope can be sustained.

References

Acemoglu, D. and J. Robinson (2013) *Why nations fail: The origin of power, prosperity and poverty.* London: Profile Books.

Adesina, J., Y. Graham and A. Olukoshi (eds) (2006) *Africa and development challenges in the new millennium: The NEPAD debate.* Dakar, London and Pretoria: CODESRIA, Zed Press and UNISA Press.

Adetula, V. (1992) "Three decades of ECA in Africa: An appraisal." *Quarterly Journal of Administration* 27(1): 37-52.

Adetula, V. (1997) *Claude Ake and Democracy in Africa: A Tribute.* African Centre for Democratic Governance, Afrigov Monograph No. 4.

Adetula, V. (2003) "Economic and socio-cultural networks in West Africa: What prospects for the development of transnational civil society?" In *Civil society partners for democracy: ICSF-2003 Documents*, Ulaanbaatar, Mongolia; ICSF pp.136–42.

Adetula, V. (2005) "Development, conflict and peacebuilding in Africa" in Shedrack Gaya Best (ed.) *Introduction to peace and conflict studies in West Africa.* Ibadan: University for Peace/Spectrum Books, pp. 383–405.

Adetula, V. (2008) "The role of sub-regional integration schemes in conflict prevention and management in Africa: A framework for working peace system." In Alfred Nhema and Paul Zeleza (eds) *The resolution of African conflicts: The management of conflict resolution and post conflict reconstruction.* Addis Ababa/Oxford/Athens: OSSREA/James Currey/UNISA Press/ Ohio University Press, pp. 9–21.

Adetula, V. (2009) "West African labour migrants and national security in Nigeria." In Michael Ben Arrous and Lazare Ki-Zerbo (eds) *Etudes africaines de geographie par le bas African Studies in Geography from Below.* Dakar: CODESRIA, pp. 269–95.

Adetula, V. (2010) "NEPAD and Africa: EU strategic partnership agreement." In Osita Eze and Amadu Sesay (eds) *Europe and Africa in the 21ˢᵗ century.* Lagos: Nigerian Institute of International Affairs, pp. 99–126.

Adetula, V. (2011) "Measuring democracy and 'good governance' in Africa: A critique of assumptions and methods." In Kwandiwe Kondlo and Chinenyengozi Ejiogu (eds) *Africa in focus: Governance in the 21st Century.* Pretoria: Human Science Research Council, pp. 10–25.

Adetula, V. (2014) "Mediators or meddlers: Resource factor as a constraints in resolving African conflicts" in Bola Akinterinwa (ed.) *Organization of African Unity/African Union at 50.* Vol. 1. *Challenges and prospects of self-reliance in Africa.* Lagos: Nigerian Institute of International Affairs, pp. 301–44.

African Union (2010) *African peace and security architecture (APSA): 2010 Assessment Study* Addis Ababa: AU Commission.

Alao, A. (2000) "The role of African regional and sub-regional Organisations in conflict prevention and resolution" *New Issues in Refugee Research, Working Paper* No. 23, July.http://www.unhcr.org/cgibin/texis/vtx/home/opendocPDFViewer.htm l?docid=3ae6a0c88&query=Abiodun Alao (Accessed 20 April 2014).

Aljazeera America "Is CAR on the verge of genocide?" http://www.aljazeera.com/programmes/insidestory/2013/12/car-verge-genocide-201312683955578607.htm (Accessed 15 January 2014).

Allansson, M., M. Sollenberg and L. Themnér (2013) "Armed conflict in the wake of the Arab Spring." In *SIPRI Yearbook 2013: Armaments, disarmament and international security.* Oxford: Oxford University Press, pp. 17–40.

Allouche, J. (2014) "Undercurrents of violence: Why Sierra Leone's political settlement is not working." IDS Policy Briefing 48.

Anyang' Nyongo, P., A. Ghirmazion and D. Lamba (eds) (2002) *New Partnership for Africa's Development, NEPAD: A New Path?* Nairobi: Heinrich Böll Foundation.

Armah-Attoh, D., E. Gyimah-Boadi and A. Chikwanha (2007) "Corruption and institutional trust in Africa: Implications for democratic development." Afrobarometer Working Papers No. 81.

Ascher, W. and N. Mirovitskaya (2013) "Development strategies and the evolution of violence in Africa." In W. Ascher and N. Mirovitskaya (eds) *The economic roots of conflict and cooperation in Africa.* New York: Palgrave Macmillan. Bam, S. (2012) "Foreword." In L. Gelot, L. Gelot and C. de Coning (eds) *Supporting African Peace Operations.* Nordic Africa Institute Policy Dialogue No. 8, pp. 8–9.

Bratton M. and N. Van de Walle (1997) "Neopatrimonial rule in Africa." In M. Bratton and N. Van de Walle (eds), *Democratic experiments in Africa: Regime transitions in comparative perspective.* Cambridge: Cambridge University Press.

Brewer, J. (2010) *Peace processes: A sociological approach.* Cambridge: Polity Press.

Bruck, T. (2013) "An economist's perspective on security, conflict and peace research." In *SIPRI Yearbook 2013: Armaments, disarmament and international security.* Oxford: Oxford University Press, pp. 1–13.

Butty, J. (2010) "A new study finds death toll in Congo war too high", VOA News, 21 January. http://www.globalsecurity.org/military/library/news/2010/01/mil-100121-voa05.htm (Accessed 15 January 2014).

Cheru, F. (2002) *African renaissance: Roadmaps to the challenge of globalization.* London and Cape Town: Zed Books and David Philip.

Claude, I. (1971) *Swords into plowshares.* New York: Random House.

Collier, C. (2009) *Wars, guns, and votes: Democracy in dangerous laces* New York: Harper Collins.

Collier, P. (2000) *Economic causes of civil conflict and their implications for policy.* Washington DC: World Bank.

Collier, P. and A. Hoeffler (2004) "Greed and grievance in civil war." *Oxford Economic Papers* 56(4): 478–95.

Collier, P., A. Hoeffler and D. Rohner (2009) "Beyond greed and grievance: Feasibility and civil war" *Oxford Economic Papers* 61(1): 1-27.

Daniel, D., B. Hayes and C. Oudraat (1998) *Coercive inducement and the containment of international crises.* Washington DC: US Institute of Peace Press.

De Waal, A. (2013) "Syria: a view from Africa." http://africanarguments. org/2013/09/12/syria-a-view-from-africa-by-alex-de-waal/ (Accessed 15 January 2014).

Deng, F. (1996) *Sovereignty as responsibility: Conflict management in Africa.* Washington DC: Brookings Institution.

Dersso, S. (2011) "Reflections on the adequacy and potential of the APSA for responding to popular uprisings." In I. Souare and B. Mesfin (eds) *A critical look at the 2011 North African revolutions and their implications* Pretoria: Institute for Security Studies, pp. 35–40.

Dersso, S. (2013) "The best option to settle the CAR Crisis." http://www-aljazeera. com/indepth/opinion/2013/12/k (Accessed 20 January 2014).

Deutsch, K. (1978) *The analysis of international relations.* Englewood Cliffs NJ: Prentice-Hall.

Diamond, L. (1996) "Is the third wave over?" *Journal of Democracy* 7(3): 20–37.

Dieter, H., G. Lamb and H. Melber (2002) "Prospects for regional co-operation in Southern Africa." In Regionalism and regionalism and regional integration in Africa: A debate of current aspects and issue, Nordic Africa Institute Discussion Paper no. 11.

Dulani, B. (2013) After a Decade of Growth in Africa, Little Change in Poverty at the Grassroots. Afrobarometer Policy Brief No.1, October.

Dundon, J. (2013) "Global trends in peace operations." In *SIPRI Yearbook 2013: Armaments, disarmament and international security.* Oxford: Oxford University Press, pp. 63–75.

Ellis, S. (2009) "West Africa's International Drug Trade." *African Affairs* 108(431): 171–96.

Fahlén, M. (2015) "The African Union mission in Somali: Toward a new vision of regional peacekeeping." In Peter Wallensteen and Anders Bjurner (eds) *Regional Organizations and Peacemaking: Challengers to the UN?* London: Routledge, pp. 179–93.

Ferguson, N. (2003) "Hegemony or Empire?" *Foreign Affairs* September/October, pp. 154–61.

Haas, E. (1958) *The Uniting of Europe.* Stanford: Stanford University Press.

Haas, E. (1961) "International integration: The European and the universal process," *International Organization* 15(3): 366–92.

Haas, E. (1970) "The study of regional integration: Reflections on joy and anguish of pretheorizing." *International Organization* 24(4): 607–46.

Haas, E. (2004) *The uniting of Europe: Political, social, and economic forces, 1950–1957.* Notre Dame: University of Notre Dame Press.

Hegre, H., J. Karlsen, H.M. Nygård, H. Strand and H. Urdal (2013) "Predicting armed conflict, 2011–2050." *International Studies Quarterly* 57(2): 250–70.

Herbst, J. (2000) "Western and African peacekeepers: Motives and opportunities." In John W. Harbeson and Donald Rothchild (eds) *Africa in world politics. The African state system in flux.* Boulder CO: Westview, pp. 308–28.

Hillen, J. (1998) *Blue helmets: The strategy of UN military operations.* London: Brassey's.

Homer-Dixon, T. (1999) *Environmental, Scarcity, and Violence.* Princeton NJ: Princeton University Press.

Hull, C., E. Skeppstsröm and K. Sörensson (2011) Patchwork for Peace: Regional Capabilities for Peace and Security in eastern Africa. Swedish Defence Research Agency Report No FOI-R-3048-SE, September.

Hutchful, E. (1998) "Demilitarization in Africa: An Update." Discussion paper prepared for Conference on Leadership Challenges of Demilitarization in Africa, organised by Center for Peace and Reconciliation, in conjunction with the Africa Leadership Forum and the United Nations Development Program (UNDP), Arusha, Tanzania, 22–24 July.

Jeng, A. (2012) *Peacebuilding in the African Union: Law, Philosophy and Practice.* Cambridge: Cambridge University Press.

Käihkö, I. and M. Utas (2014) "The crisis in CAR: Navigating myths and interests." *Africa Spectrum* 49(1): 69–77.

Kreutz, J. (2012) *Dismantling the conflict trap: Essays on civil war resolution and relapse.* Uppsala: Department of Peace and Conflict Research, Uppsala University, Report No. 96.

Ladsous, H. (2014) "UN peacekeeping operations in Africa: Change in 2013 and priorities for 2014." Speech by UN Under-Secretary General for the Department of Peacekeeping Operations, Chatham House, 13 January.

Lieber, R. (1973) *Theory and world politics.* London: Allen and Unwin.

Lindberg, L., and S. Scheingold (1970) *Europe's would-be polity: Patterns of change in European community.* Englewood Cliffs: Prentice Hall.

Mandela, N. (1998) Address of the President of the Republic of South Africato the Summit Meeting of the Organization of African Unity Heads of State and Government, Ouagadougou, Burkina Faso, 8 June.

McNamara, R. (1991) "The post-Cold War world: Implications for military expenditure in the developing countries." Proceedings of the World Bank Annual Conference on Development Economics, World Bank.

Mehler, A., H. Melber and K. Walraven (eds) (2013) *Africa Yearbook,* Vol.9, *Politics, Economy and Society South of the Sahara in 2012.* Leiden: Brill.

Melander, E., M. Öberg and J. Hall (2006) *The new wars debate revisited: An empirical evaluation of the atrociousness of 'new wars'.* Uppsala: Department of Peace and Conflict Research, Uppsala University, Report No. 9.

Mine, Y., F. Stewart, SFakuda-Parr and T. Mkandawire (2013) *Preventing violent conflict in Africa: Inequalities, perception and institutions.*Palgrave Macmillan.

Mitrany, D. (1966) *A Working Peace System.* Chicago: Quadrangle Books.

Museveni, Y.K. (2001) *Why Uganda, Nigeria or the African Union?* National War College, Abuja, Nigeria, Distinguished Lecture Series No. 3.

New Partnership for Africa's Development (NEPAD) (2001) *The New partnership for Africa's development.* http://www. dfa.gov.za/events. Nepad.pdf (Accessed 30 September 2003).

Nyuykonge, C. (2012) "Post-conflict reconstruction and the resurgence of 'resolved' territorial conflicts: Examining the DRC peace process ." *Ubuntu* 1(1 and 2): 111–35.

Nzongola-Ntalaja, G. (2002) "Good Governance and Conflict Management: Will the African Union Make a Difference?" Forum Evening, CCM's Norwegian Peacebuilding Empowerment Programme, Oslo, 4 September.

Oakley, R.B., M.J. Dziedzic and E.M. Goldberg (eds) (1998) *Policing the new world order: Peace operations and public security.* Washington DC: National Defense University Press.

O'Brien, P. and A. Cleese (2002) *Two hegemonies: Britain 1846-1914 and the United States 1941-2001.* Aldershot: Ashgate.

Ohlson, T. (ed.) (2012) *From intra-state war to durable peace: Conflict and its resolution in Africa after the Cold War.* Dordrecht: Republic of Letters Publishing.

Oppong, R. (2011) *Legal Aspects of Economic Integration in Africa.* Cambridge: Cambridge University Press.

Östby, G. (2013) "Inequality and political violence: A review of the literature." *International Area Studies Review* 16(206): 206–31.

Packer, C. and D. Rukare (2002) "The new African Union and its Constitutive Act." *American Journal of International Law* 96(2): 365–79.

Saferworld (2011) *China's growing role in African peace and security.* Saferworld Report

Sandholtz, W. and A. Sweet (1997) "European integration and supranational governance." *Journal of European Public Policy* 4: 297–317.

Sanu, E.O. and V.A.O. Adetula, (1989) "The Lomé Convention: Growth and Hindrances to ECOWAS." *Economic Quarterly* 24(2): 20–3.

Scheingold, S.A. (2013) *The rule of law in European integration: The path of the Schuman Plan.* Malcolm M. Feeley (University of California at Berkeley) : Quid Pro Books.

Schmitter, P. (1969) "Three neo-functional hypotheses about international integration." *International Organization* 23(1): 161–6.

Schori, P. (2015) "ECOWAS and the AU in Cooperation with the Unite Case of Cote d' Ivoire." In Peter Wallensteen and Anders Bjurner (eds) *Regional Organizations and Peacemaking: Challengers to the UN?* London: Routledge, pp. 160–78.

Sesay, A (2002) "The role of ECOWAS in promoting peace and security in West Africa." *DPMN Bulletin* IX (3), June. http://www.dpmf.org/role-ecowas-peace-amadu.html (Accessed 30 September 2002).

SIPRI (2013) *SIPRI Yearbook 2013: Armaments, disarmament* and *international security.* Oxford: Oxford University Press.

Snow, D. (1996) *Uncivil wars: International security and the new internal conflicts* Boulder CO: Lynne Rienner.

Stensson, E. (2008) The African Union's operations in the Comoros, MAES and Operation Democracy. Swedish Defence Research Agency Report No FOI-R-2659-SE, September.

Swanström, N. (2002) *Regional cooperation and conflict management: lessons from the Pacific Rim.* Uppsala: Department of Peace and Conflict Research, Uppsala University, Report No. 64.

Sweet A., W. Sandholtz and N. Fligstein (2001) *The institutionalization of Europe.* Oxford: Oxford University Press.

Tandia, A. (2012) "How African civil wars hibernate: The warring communities of the Senegal/Guinea Bissau Borderlands in the face of the Casamance forgotten civil war and the Bissau-Guinean State Failure." *Ubuntu* 1 (1 and 2): 36–51.

Themnér, L. and P. Wallensteen (2013) "Patterns of organized violence, 2002–11." In *SIPRI Yearbook 2013: Armaments, disarmament and international security.* Oxford: Oxford University Press, pp. 41–50.

Tschirgi, N. (2003) *Peacebuilding as the link between security and development: Is the window of opportunity closing?* New York: International Peace Academy Studies in Security and Development.

US Department of State National Counterterrorism Centre (2012) "Country reports on terrorism 2011", July 31 http//:www.state.gov./j/ct/rls/crt/2011/195555.htm (Accessed 10 January 2014).

UNECA (2013) *African Governance Report III: Elections and the management of diversity* Oxford: Oxford University Press.

Utas, M. (2012) "Introduction: Bigmanity and network governance in Africa." In Mats Utas (ed.) *African conflicts and informal power: Big men and networks.* Uppsala and London: Nordiska Afrikainstitutet and Zed Books, pp. 1–31.

Wallensteen, P. (2012) "Regional peacebuilding: A new challenge." *New Routes* 17(4): 3–6.

Wallensteen, P. (2001) Conflict prevention through development cooperation: An inventory of recent findings with implications for international development cooperation. Department of Peace and Conflict Research, Uppsala University, Report No. 59.

Williams, P. (2006) "The African Union: Prospects for regional peacekeeping after Burundi and Sudan." *Review of African Political Economy* 33(108): 352–7.

World Bank (2013) *Nigeria Economic Report.* http://www-wds.worldbank.org/external/default/WDSContentServer/WDSP/IB/2013/05/14/000333037_20130514101211/Rendered/PDF/776840WP0Niger0Box0342041B00PUBLIC0.pdf (Accessed 20 January 2014).

Young, J. (2012) *The fate of Sudan: Origins and consequences of a flawed peace process.* London: Zed Books.

Zacher, M. (1979) *International conflicts and collective security, 1946-77.* New York: Praeger.

CURRENT AFRICAN ISSUES PUBLISHED BY THE INSTITUTE

Recent issues in the series are available electronically
for download free of charge www.nai.uu.se

1981

1. *South Africa, the West and the Frontline States. Report from a Seminar.*

2. Maja Naur, *Social and Organisational Change in Libya.*

3. *Peasants and Agricultural Production in Africa. A Nordic Research Seminar. Follow-up Reports and Discussions.*

1985

4. Ray Bush & S. Kibble, *Destabilisation in Southern Africa, an Overview.*

5. Bertil Egerö, *Mozambique and the Southern African Struggle for Liberation.*

1986

6. Carol B.Thompson, *Regional Economic Polic under Crisis Condition. Southern African Development.*

1989

7. Inge Tvedten, *The War in Angola, Internal Conditions for Peace and Recovery.*

8. Patrick Wilmot, *Nigeria's Southern Africa Policy 1960–1988.*

1990

9. Jonathan Baker, *Perestroika for Ethiopia: In Search of the End of the Rainbow?*

10. Horace Campbell, *The Siege of Cuito Cuanavale.*

1991

11. Maria Bongartz, *The Civil War in Somalia. Its genesis and dynamics.*

12. Shadrack B.O. Gutto, *Human and People's Rights in Africa. Myths, Realities and Prospects.*

13. Said Chikhi, Algeria. *From Mass Rebellion to Workers' Protest.*

14. Bertil Odén, *Namibia's Economic Links to South Africa.*

1992

15. Cervenka Zdenek, *African National Congress Meets Eastern Europe. A Dialogue on Common Experiences.*

1993

16. Diallo Garba, *Mauritania–The Other Apartheid?*

1994

17. Zdenek Cervenka and Colin Legum, *Can National Dialogue Break the Power of Terror in Burundi?*

18. Erik Nordberg and Uno Winblad, *Urban Environmental Health and Hygiene in Sub-Saharan Africa.*

1996

19. Chris Dunton and Mai Palmberg, *Human Rights and Homosexuality in Southern Africa.*

1998

20. Georges Nzongola-Ntalaja, *From Zaire to the Democratic Republic of the Congo.*

1999

21. Filip Reyntjens, *Talking or Fighting? Political Evolution in Rwanda and Burundi, 1998–1999.*

22. Herbert Weiss, *War and Peace in the Democratic Republic of the Congo.*

2000

23. Filip Reyntjens, *Small States in an Unstable Region – Rwanda and Burundi, 1999–2000.*

2001

24. Filip Reyntjens, *Again at the Crossroads: Rwanda and Burundi, 2000–2001.*

25. Henning Melber, *The New African Initiative and the African Union. A Preliminary Assessment and Documentation.*

2003

26. Dahilon Yassin Mohamoda, *Nile Basin Cooperation. A Review of the Literature.*

2004

27. Henning Melber (ed.), *Media, Public Discourse and Political Contestation in Zimbabwe.*

28. Georges Nzongola-Ntalaja, *From Zaire to the Democratic Republic of the Congo.* (Second and Revised Edition)

2005

29. Henning Melber (ed.), *Trade, Development, Cooperation – What Future for Africa?*

30. Kaniye S.A. Ebeku, *The Succession of Faure Gnassingbe to the Togolese Presidency – An International Law Perspective.*

31. J.V. Lazarus, C. Christiansen, L. Rosendal Østergaard, L.A. Richey, Models for Life – Advancing antiretroviral therapy in sub-Saharan Africa.

2006

32. Charles Manga Fombad & Zein Kebonang, *AU, NEPAD and the APRM – Democratisation Efforts Explored.* (Ed. H. Melber.)

33. P.P. Leite, C. Olsson, M. Schöldtz, T. Shelley, P. Wrange, H. Corell and K. Scheele, *The Western Sahara Conflict – The Role of Natural Resources in Decolonization.* (Ed. Claes Olsson)

2007

34. Jassey, Katja and Stella Nyanzi, *How to Be a "Proper" Woman in the Times of HIV and AIDS.*

35. M. Lee, H. Melber, S. Naidu and I. Taylor, *China in Africa.* (Compiled by Henning Melber)

36. Nathaniel King, *Conflict as Integration. Youth Aspiration to Personhood in the Teleology of Sierra Leone's 'Senseless War'.*

2008

37. Aderanti Adepoju, *Migration in sub-Saharan Africa.*

38. Bo Malmberg, *Demography and the development potential of sub-Saharan Africa.*

39. Johan Holmberg, *Natural resources in sub-Saharan Africa: Assets and vulnerabilities.*

40. Arne Bigsten and Dick Durevall, *The African economy and its role in the world economy.*

41. Fantu Cheru, *Africa's development in the 21st century: Reshaping the research agenda.*

2009

42. Dan Kuwali, *Persuasive Prevention. Towards a Principle for Implementing Article 4(h) and R2P by the African Union.*

43. Daniel Volman, *China, India, Russia and the United States. The Scramble for African Oil and the Militarization of the Continent.*

2010

44. Mats Hårsmar, *Understanding Poverty in Africa? A Navigation through Disputed Concepts, Data and Terrains.*

2011

45. Sam Maghimbi, Razack B. Lokina and Mathew A. Senga, *The Agrarian Question in Tanzania? A State of the Art Paper.*

46. William Minter, *African Migration, Global Inequalities, and Human Rights. Connecting the Dots.*

47. Musa Abutudu and Dauda Garuba, *Natural Resource Governance and EITI Implementation in Nigeria.*

48. Ilda Lindell, *Transnational Activism Networks and Gendered Gatekeeping. Negotiating Gender in an African Association of Informal Workers.*

2012

49. Terje Oestigaard, *Water Scarcity and Food Security along the Nile. Politics, population increase and climate change.*

50. David Ross Olanya, *From Global Land Grabbing for Biofuels to Acquisitions of AfricanWater for Commercial Agriculture.*

2013

51. Gessesse Dessie, *Favouring a Demonised Plant. Khat and Ethiopian smallholder enterprise.*

52. Boima Tucker, *Musical Violence. Gangsta Rap and Politics in Sierra Leone.*

53. David Nilsson, *Sweden-Norway at the Berlin Conference 1884–85. History, national identity-making and Sweden's relations with Africa.*

54. Pamela K. Mbabazi, *The Oil Industry in Uganda; A Blessing in Disguise or an all Too Familiar Curse? Paper presented at the Claude Ake Memorial Lecture.*

55. Måns Fellesson & Paula Mählck, *Academics on the Move. Mobility and Institutional Change in the Swedish Development Support to Research Capacity Buildiing in Mozambique.*

56. Clementina Amankwaah. *Election-Related Violence: The Case of Ghana.*

57. Farida Mahgoub. *Current Status of Agriculture and Future Challenges in Sudan.*

58. Emy Lindberg. *Youth and the Labour Market in Liberia – on history, state structures and spheres of informalities.*

59. Marianna Wallin. *Resettled for Development. The Case of New Halfa Agricultural Scheme, Sudan.*

60. Joseph Watuleke. *The Role of Food Banks in Food Security in Uganda. The Case of the Hunger Project Food Bank, Mbale Epicentre.*

61. Victor A.O. Adetula. *African Conflicts, Development and Regional Organisations in the Post-Cold War International System. The Annual Claude Ake Memoral Lecture Uppsala, Sweden 30 January 2014.*

CLAUDE AKE MEMORIAL PAPER SERIES

Published by Uppsala University and the Department of Peace and Conflict Research
Recent issues in the series are available electronically for download free of charge
www.pcr.uu.se/research/publications/CAMP/

1. Jinadu, L. Adele : Explaining & Managing Ethnic Conflict in Africa: Towards a Cultural Theory of Democracy (2007).

2. Obi, Cyril I: No Choice, But Democracy: Prising the People out of Politics in Africa? (2008).

3. Sesay, Amadu: The African Union: Forward March or About Face-Turn? (2008).

4. Boafo-Arthur, Kwame: Democracy and Stability in West Africa: The Ghanaian Experience (2008).

5. Villa-Vicencio, Charles: Where the Old Meets the New: Transitional Justice, Peacebuilding and Traditional Reconciliation Practices in Africa (2009).

6. Mohamed, Adam Azzain: Evaluating the Darfur Peace Agreement: A Call for an Alternative Approach to Crisis Management (2009).

7. Mbabazi, Pamela K: The Oil Industry in Uganda; A Blessing in Disguise or an all Too Familiar Curse? (2013).

8. Victor A.O. Adetula. African Conflicts, Development and Regional Organisations in the Post-Cold War International System (2015).

www.ingramcontent.com/pod-product-compliance
Lightning Source LLC
Chambersburg PA
CBHW080208300326
41934CB00039B/3423